SOCIAL ISSUES, JUSTICE AND STATUS

SOCIOECONOMIC STATUS

INFLUENCES, DISPARITIES AND CURRENT ISSUES

Social Issues, Justice and Status

Additional books in this series can be found on Nova's website
under the Series tab.

Additional e-books in this series can be found on Nova's website
under the eBooks tab.

SOCIAL ISSUES, JUSTICE AND STATUS

SOCIOECONOMIC STATUS

INFLUENCES, DISPARITIES AND CURRENT ISSUES

GEOFFREY PERKINS
EDITOR

nova publishers
New York

Library of Congress Cataloging-in-Publication Data

ISBN: 978-1-63485-326-2

Published by Nova Science Publishers, Inc. † New York

CONTENTS

PREFACE

This book provides research on the influences, disparities and current issues of socioeconomic status (SES). Chapter One discusses socio-economic status, inequality and academic achievement. Chapter Two reviews literature on socioeconomic variables that predict a child's executive functioning and possible contextual and cognitive variables mediating this association. Chapter Three examines socioeconomic and racial disparities in child health and health outcomes. Chapter Four analyzes attitudes toward poverty and the government safety net programs in relationship to income and party affiliation, and investigates theories to better understand the polarized attitudes toward socioeconomic status, inequality and poverty in America. Chapter Five provides a review of three different studies which underpin the proposal of the benefits and pitfalls of high SES. Chapter Six reports the findings of two questionnaire surveys focusing on the effects of socioeconomic status and trait self-control on seeking relationships.

In: Socioeconomic Status
Editor: Geoffrey Perkins

ISBN: 978-1-63485-326-2

Chapter 1

SOCIO-ECONOMIC STATUS, INEQUALITY AND ACADEMIC ACHIEVEMENT

Ming Ming Chiu*
Educational Psychology and Research Methodology,
Purdue University, West Lafayette, IN, US

ABSTRACT

Families with more education, higher incomes or higher social status (socio-economic status or SES) than other families can use their superior resources to help their children obtain higher academic achievement, while greater SES inequality reduces the academic achievement of not only poorer students but also students overall. Higher SES families have more capital (human, financial, social and cultural) and can provide their children with more educational resources and learning opportunities. These higher SES children can then capitalize on these additional resources and opportunities to learn more. Furthermore, students in higher SES families often attend schools with more resources, which support higher academic achievement. Lastly, students in these families can often obtain a larger share of school or country resources to aid their own learning, even though this inequality can hurt the overall achievement of the school or the country. SES inequality has overall negative effects on all students' learning, both rich and poor, due to fewer educational resources and inefficient resource allocation. In countries

* Purdue University, 5156 Beering Hall, 100 North Street, West Lafayette, IN, 47907, United States. Email: mingmingchiu@gmail.com.

with fewer educational resources, students learn less overall. Likewise, when resources are inefficiently allocated to richer students who do not need them as much as poorer students, overall student achievement is lower.

Keywords: socio-economic status, inequality, academic achievement, family, country, school, culture, student, learning

INTRODUCTION

Families whose members are more educated or earn higher incomes have higher social status (*socio-economic status* or *SES*) and can provide their children with more educational resources and learning opportunities (Chiu & Khoo, 2005). These children can then capitalize on these additional resources and opportunities to learn more. Specifically, a student whose family SES is 10% higher than average has 3% higher academic achievement than other students on average (see Sirin's [2005] meta-analysis).

Furthermore, students in higher SES families often attend schools with more resources, which supports higher academic achievement (Chiu, 2013a). These students can often obtain a larger share of school or country resources to aid their own learning, even though this inequality can hurt the overall achievement of the school or the country (Chiu & Khoo, 2005). Specifically, countries with greater economic inequality have fewer educational resources overall and less efficient resource allocation, both of which reduce overall student achievement (Chiu, 2015).

FAMILY

Families differ with respect to their human capital (e.g., education), financial capital (wealth), social capital (social network resources) and cultural capital (knowledge of dominant culture and society, Chiu, 2013b). As a result, children in different families often do not have access to the same educational resources and consequently enter school with different skills and competencies.

Human Capital

Families with more human capital can create more conducive physical environments, more appropriate reward/discipline structures, and engage in more supportive activities to help socialize their children into society (Chiu & Khoo, 2005). In particular, families with highly educated parents tend to appreciate and buy (or make) higher quality physical resources, such as rooms for quiet study and age-appropriate books for children. By doing so, they create stimulating and reflective learning environments.

Families with more human capital also create suitable reward and discipline structures (Chiu & Joh, 2015). Parents with more human capital clarify and organize their children's time to study at regular times, praise them for exerting effort and help them understand the consequences of not putting effort into their studies. By doing so, these families foster compassionate, social interactions; diligent, academic study; and joyful, creative expression. Also, these families with more human capital are more likely than other families to encourage children to consider other people's different preferences and perspectives and to discuss why some behaviors were unacceptable after age-appropriate time for reflection (time-outs). As a result, these students are better prepared to study diligently, behave properly in school and learn more.

Families with more human capital can also help socialize children through both education-specific activities and general activities (Chiu & Chow, 2015a). For example, a parent might talk with a child about school matters such as homework, recent political events, books, and so on. They can also chat during dinner, tell one another stories, play games, wash dishes together, or generally spend time together. Through these interactions, family members can serve as role models, ask provoking questions or give explicit instructions, all of which can help children learn linguistic, cognitive, behavioral and social skills. Much communication occurs in the form of individual or jointly-constructed stories, precursors to reading literacy. These stories and other conversations help children develop language skills and enrich their vocabulary. Highly-educated family members, especially parents, can monitor and supervise children more actively and have more information and skills than other parents to teach their children.

Family members' conversations with children also improve their understanding of different perspectives, their problem solving and their organization skills (*metacognitive skills,* Chiu, 2013c). During dinner conversations, for example, children can learn about other family members' perspectives and engage in critical thinking and problem solving about others' concerns. Children can also learn to organize and shift among many dinner activities --asking for, serving, and eating food; planning family activities; following societal norms of pleasant conversations, and so on. By engaging in these activities, children develop enhanced cognitive capacities that can help them approach intellectual matters in a more reflective, open, considered, and sustained way, thereby improving their academic performance.

Family members can also create organizational structures and routines to help children develop their metacognitive skills (Chiu, 2013c). For example, family members can help children develop positive routines and habits with carefully placed posters, such as a bedroom door poster of a toothbrush to remind children to brush their teeth before going to bed. Furthermore, standardized procedures for resolving disputes, such listening to each person's entire narrative of a contested incident and asking information questions, can help children develop self-regulation skills and discipline to behave properly with not only family members at home but also classmates, teachers and staff at school.

Financial Capital

Families with more human capital often have greater income and wealth (*financial capital*), which they can use to give their children more resources and activities (Chiu & Khoo, 2005). For example, richer families often give their children more physical resources (quiet study room, computers, books, etc.), thereby creating a richer learning environment. These families also tend to appreciate and buy higher quality resources, such as age-appropriate books and computer software for their children. Buying their children many educational resources also highlights stronger family commitment to their learning. Furthermore, non-educational resources such as expensive clothes serve as status symbols that can enhance children's status among their peers, which helps them make friends at school and have more positive attitudes about school. Richer families can also pay for stimulating activities, such as summer camps and travel to other countries, to enhance their children's learning experiences.

Cultural Capital

Families with more human capital or financial capital may also have more cultural possessions, cultural experiences and time to give children more opportunities to learn these cultural resources, knowledge, skills and values, which helps them fit into the culture of their family, school, and local community (*cultural capital*, Chiu & Chow, 2010). Cultural possessions at home (e.g., paintings, poetry, etc.) can exemplify the importance of one's culture and facilitate family communication about cultural values and norms.

During cultural conversations, family members can model appropriate societal behaviors and explain cultural norms to help their children learn the cultural values of their family, school, and society (Chiu, 2013c). Specifically, these cultural conversations can help children better understand teachers' and classmates' expectations in school so that they can behave appropriately and build better relationships with them. By doing so, families can help children understand and adapt to other people's expectations of them.

Combined with their cognitive skills, metacognitive skills and social skills, children's adaptation to others' expectations helps them build friendships more easily (Chiu, 2013b.) Supported by teachers and children, these children with more cultural capital might receive more learning opportunities, be more motivated, learn more, and be more successful in school.

Social Capital

Higher SES families are more likely than lower SES families have larger and richer social networks of family, friends and acquaintances (*social capital*, Lareau, 2001). Connecting a child with their family members' networks can add to a child's social capital.

Furthermore, the members of high SES families' extensive social networks can offer additional complementary material, human, social and cultural capital to support their children's learning (Chiu, 2013b). For example, relatives or friends may lend an interesting book to a child to read, and then discuss it upon its return. As noted above, family communication helps children develop linguistic skills, including discourse skills that help children communicate with both their peers and teachers. Children who communicate better are more liked and more accepted by their peer group, resulting in a larger network of friends and acquaintances. Furthermore, educated members of the network of a child's family can help acculturate the child to academic conversation norms and expectations that facilitate their understanding and use of them in school compared to other students.

Higher SES Students in Richer Schools

School systems based on open markets or cronyism (rather on random allocation) enable higher SES students to attend schools with high quality physical resources, effective teachers, and high SES schoolmates (e.g., Chile, Germany, Indonesia). In open markets, elite private schools charge high tuitions to cater to rich students, using the tuition to hire skilled staff (principals, teachers, etc.) and buy superior educational resources (computers, labs, etc.; Darling-Hammond & Post, 2000). Similarly, locally-funded public schools (e.g., via neighborhood taxes) serve as indirect open markets, in which richer families move to richer neighborhoods with better funded schools (Hoxby, 2001).

In unequal school systems, the resources in each school often differ widely. In the United States for example, funding per student in one school can be 25 times higher than in another as a result of government preferential funding, private school alumni donations, and school budgets funded by local taxes (Rothstein, 2000). Better schools often have better physical conditions, more educational materials (books, computers) and better teachers than other schools (Fuller & Clarke, 1994). These schools often have higher teacher-to-student ratios and better-qualified teachers (e.g., university degrees, Rivkin, Hanushek, & Cain, 2005). Superior teachers use more effective teaching processes, maintain better student discipline and relationships with their students –all of which are linked to higher student achievement (e.g., Ma & Willms, 2004; Rowan, Correnti, & Miller, 2002; Willms & Somer, 2001). Hence, students in superior schools often have more opportunities to learn and capitalize on them to learn more (Chiu, 2015). Teachers also tend to give higher SES students more attention compared to lower SES students (*privilege bias*), which tends to increase higher SES student achievement and reduce lower SES student achievement (Chiu & Khoo, 2005).

Open markets also tend to cluster elite housing together in elite neighborhoods in many countries. As a result, high SES students often live together in the same neighborhoods and attend the same schools, separating them from low SES students who cluster together in poorer neighborhoods (schoolmate inequality, Chiu & Khoo, 2005).

Students can benefit from these privileged schoolmates' family capital, material resources, diverse experiences, and high academic expectations (Pritchett, 2001). Privileged classmates tend to help a student understand and appreciate the societal and cultural value of schooling, thereby contributing to a class or school culture of higher academic achievement and better discipline

(Chiu & McBride-Chang, 2006). As a result, low SES students often benefit from high SES classmates' greater learning resources (Chiu & Chow, 2015b). In countries with greater schoolmate inequality however, low SES students are less likely to have high SES schoolmates.

Meanwhile, cronyism also concentrates skilled staff and educational resources in elite schools, to which families with more social capital (e.g., government officials) send their children (Lloyd & Blanc, 1996). In less equal school systems, privileged parents have more incentives to use their financial and/or social capital to enroll their children into better schools. School inequality is substantially greater in poorer countries (specifically, those with less than $16,000 per capita gross domestic product in 1990 US Dollars, Gamoran & Long, 2006).

Higher SES Students within a School

In addition to attending richer schools, high SES students can also exploit greater access to resources within a school. Within school inequality includes unequal resource allocation, tracking, and steep status hierarchies. Privileged parents can leverage their superior resources to direct more educational resources for their children, leaving fewer resources for disadvantaged children. These methods might include explicit bribes of teachers (e.g., Hani, 2005), special favors through social connections with the school staff (cronyism, Lloyd & Blanc, 1996), or greater affinity with teachers due to similar social norms or cultural capital (Roscigno & Ainsworth-Darnell's, 1999 "cultural gatekeeping"). For example, after a lesson that a student liked, a parent with more social skills and cultural capital might send the teacher a thank you note and ask for study tips. As a result, the teacher might devote more attention to this student.

Furthermore, some schools (or school systems) assign students with similar past achievement scores together in a class (or a school, or a group within a class, also known as *tracking*, *ability grouping*, or *streaming*). Although tracking does not raise overall learning, it sharply increases the variance in learning (studies show non-significant or slightly negative effects on learning, while variance in achievement averages 25% higher in each country that tracks, Hanushek & Wöbmann, 2006).

Tracking is often accompanied by unequal allocation of other educational resources. Higher tracks often have richer students, superior teachers, and more educational materials. As ability grouping creates elite classes and schools, privileged parents often advocate ability grouping, and their children are often placed in high track schools, classes, or groups within a class (Opdenakker & Van Damme, 2001). Hence, high SES students tend to enroll in high-track classes (Opdenakker & Van Damme, 2001). Like students with higher SES schoolmates, students with higher SES classmates often enjoy their classmates' greater economic, social, and cultural resources. Such clustering of students by SES also facilitates targeting of school resources to richer students (Chiu & Khoo, 2005).

Teachers are often attracted to the smarter students in higher tracks. Not surprisingly, teachers teaching higher track classes often have better academic qualifications, more years of schooling, and more teaching experience than other teachers (Darling-Hammond & Post, 2000). These positive teacher characteristics are linked to more effective instructional practices in higher tracks. Compared to teachers in lower tracks, teachers in higher tracks often have better prepared lessons, teach more enthusiastically, use more complex teaching materials, teach at a faster pace, and lead more stimulating discussions (Oakes, 1990). In contrast, lower-track students receive fewer explanations and directions regarding teacher expectations and goals, reducing learning opportunities (Oakes, 1985). These distinct instructional practices might explain the differences in academic performance across tracks (Van Houtte, 2004).

Allocation of school resources also interacts with a school's status hierarchy to increase inequality. According to *status characteristics* theory, people with higher status receive more attention and other social rewards (Cohen, 1994). Cohen (p. 23) states that schools, like most institutions, have "an agreed-on rank order where it is generally felt to be better to be high than low rank" or a *status hierarchy*. In schools with "steep pyramid" status hierarchies, a small group of elite staff and students receive extra resources and social rewards, separating them from others. In contrast, schools with "gentle hill" status hierarchies share resources and social rewards more equally, so people view one another as more equal.

Steep status hierarchies sharpen the differences among staff and student and help align people's behaviours with their expectations based on perceived status differences. According to expectation states theory, status is linked to the expectation of competencies for the current activity (Chiu & Khoo, 2003). High status is conferred on people who are expected to contribute positively to a desired outcome. These expectations create different opportunities to perform and receive rewards. Members can selectively invite and defer to the views of high status members while discouraging, undervaluing, or outright ignoring those of lower status members. By doing so, members enact their expectations of high status members dominating the interaction.

Through their human capital, privileged parents can also teach their children social norms and cultural capital to create greater affinity with teachers (Bourdieu, 1993). Teachers view these students as higher status, have higher expectations of these students, and often give them more attention and assistance (Roscigno & Ainsworth-Darnell's "cultural gatekeeping," 1999). According to Hallinan and Kubitschek (1999), higher teacher expectations also tend to boost student confidence, resulting in greater goal attainment. In contrast, teachers with low expectations tend to give lower status students, tasks that do not sufficiently challenge them, often resulting in both lower motivation and less learning. Likewise, students can also enact these status expectations to favor high status classmates over low status classmates during academic discussions or social interactions, either inside or outside of class (Cohen, 1994).

INEQUALITY

Country inequality reduces student learning and widens the achievement gap. When country inequality (e.g., Gini) is 10% higher than average, students score 2% lower in science, 1% lower in mathematics, and 1% lower in reading than other students, controlling for total resources in a study of fifteen-year-olds in 41 countries (Chiu & Khoo, 2005). In countries with greater inequality, the lowest socio-economic status (SES) students' scores are much lower than those of the highest SES students (Chiu, 2015). Inequality operates through micro-economic mechanisms of fewer educational resources overall (rent-seeking) and inefficient resource allocation (diminishing marginal returns) to reduce student achievement (Mankiw, 2004). *Rent-seeking* refers to using resources to acquire wealth without producing new goods or services (e.g., lobbying, fraud, extortion, etc.), resulting in less overall society productivity. *Diminishing marginal returns* occurs when increasing one type of resource yields decreasing benefits and yields inefficient allocation of resources.

Family inequality and school inequalities might reduce student achievement through different mechanisms. In this chapter, *family inequality* is defined as the income difference across households (specifically, a *Gini index*, which is suitable for non-normal distributions such as income; Mankiw, 2004). At one extreme, if all families in a country have identical income, the

Gini index = 0. At the other extreme, if one family has all the income, the Gini index = 100.

National policies can increase or reduce family inequality. For example, poor families pay more tax in a regressive tax system and less tax in a progressive tax system. In contrast, rich families pay less tax in a regressive tax system and more tax in a progressive tax system. As a result, the difference in after-tax income between poor and rich families is greater in a regressive tax system and smaller in a progressive tax system; hence, regressive tax systems tend to increase family inequality and progressive tax systems tend to reduce family inequality, ceteris paribus. In France, the progressive tax and social welfare system cuts its income inequality Gini index of 0.48 before taxes to 0.29 after taxes (OECD, 2009). Regressive taxes, corruption, and a weak legal system can increase family inequality, while progressive taxes, welfare, transparency, and health and safety standards (e.g., clean water) can reduce it (Mankiw, 2004; Merryman & Perez-Perdomo, 2007; Rothstein, 2000; Schenk & Oldman, 2007; Schubert, 2006; Williams, 2005).

As family inequality is defined across households, school inequality is defined as differences in educational resources across schools (Gamoran & Long, 2006). Two types of educational resources are educational materials and teacher quality. As with family inequality, absolute school equality of educational materials entails that every school has identical educational materials, while absolute school inequality entails that one school has all the educational materials and other schools have none (McKenzie, 2005). Likewise, similar teacher quality across schools yields greater school equality of teacher quality, while concentrating the best teachers in a few schools yield less school equality of teacher quality (McKenzie, 2005).

Countries with greater family inequality often have greater school inequalities (Rothstein, 2000). Countries with less household income inequality are more likely to have a universal public school system with teacher certification standards, which result in fewer school inequalities among students (Hanushek & Wöbmann 2006). Consider Finland versus Papua New Guinea. Finland has one of the lowest family income Gini indices in the world (0.27) and her citizens largely believe in the basic equality of each person (egalitarian cultural value, House, Hanges, Javidan, Dorfman & Gupta, 2004) and support government provision of education to all of their children (Antikainen & Luukkainen, 2008). As a result, Finland has universal, compulsory, free education with free meals and free transportation for all students. Furthermore, Finland's distribution of educational materials and teacher quality is similar across all students (in part because Finland does not separate students by achievement scores *–no tracking*).

In contrast, Papua New Guinea has one of the highest family income Gini indices in the world (0.51; CIA, 2012) and most of her citizens believe that power is naturally distributed unequally, so they do not expect equal educational opportunities for all (hierarchical cultural value, Rao, Manohar & Mellam, 2008). Unlike Finland, Papua New Guinea schools charge fees, and prestigious schools typically have more educational materials, better quality teachers and charge higher fees than other schools (UNESCO, 2010). As a result, 22% of primary school-age children in Papua New Guinea did not attend any school in 2009 (UNICEF, 2011).

MICRO-ECONOMIC MECHANISMS

Economists have shown how distribution of resources can influence productivity in *micro-economic theory*; specifically, unequal distribution of resources can reduce economic productivity through two micro-economic mechanisms, rent-seeking and diminishing marginal returns (Mankiw, 2004).

Rent-Seeking

A company can invest its resources to produce new wealth (new goods or services for sale, *profit-seeking*) or use its resources to acquire a greater share of existing wealth (without producing new goods or services, *rent-seeking* [Ilzetzki, 2011]). For example, a textbook company might invest in a new factory to produce more books (goods) to sell (profit-seeking). Or, the same company can instead pay lobbyists to persuade government officials to cut its taxes; this rent-seeking behavior seeks to increase its share of existing wealth without creating any new goods or services.

Profit-seeking behavior aims to increase social wealth, while rent-seeking behavior reduces social wealth (Murphy, Shliefer & Vishny, 1993). As profit-seeking behaviors increase goods and services, it increases social wealth. In contrast, rent-seeking behaviors spend resources without increasing goods or services; by diverting resources from potential profit-seeking behaviors (*opportunity cost*), social wealth is lower than it would be otherwise (Ilzetzki, 2011). Continuing with the above example, the textbook company has limited resources, so the amount that it invests in lobbying and other rent-seeking activities reduces its profit-seeking activities (factories, online services, etc.), resulting in less overall social wealth.

In industries with greater inequality of assets among companies, companies with more assets have greater incentive and greater means to engage in rent-seeking behavior, resulting in less social wealth (Murphy, Shliefer & Vishny, 1993). For example, sugar cane farmers in India often jointly own regional cooperative sugar processing facilities and divide the revenues from the resulting sales (Sukhtankar, 2012). In regions whose sugar cane farmers produce similar amounts of raw sugar, the revenues are divided according to the sugar cane produced by each grower, who then invests in more farm equipment to produce more sugar cane. In regions whose farmers produce sharply different amounts of sugar cane, larger sugar growers exert their greater information, influence and control to divert revenues (e.g., in Maharashtra, sugarcane cooperatives build temples and donate money to these temples, which they control), thereby paying proportionately less to smaller farmers who have less time and information to monitor the larger farmers' decisions (Banerjee, Mookherjee, Munshi & Ray, 2001). Not only do larger farmers spend their money on temples rather than farm equipment, smaller farmers are also less likely to invest in expensive farming equipment if their sugar revenues are too low. As a result, regions with greater inequality among sugar cane farmers typically produce less sugar while regions with greater equality among sugar cane farmers typically produce more sugar. In short, regions in India with greater inequality among sugar cane farmers showed more rent-seeking behavior and produced less sugar (Banerjee et al., 2001).

Diminishing Marginal Returns

When a company has a fixed set of labor and materials, increasing one type of input will often eventually yield smaller benefits (*diminishing marginal returns,* Samuelson & Nordhaus, 2009). Consider for example, a table-making company with one carpenter. The company decides to buy some hammers for her. The first hammer is extremely useful because she can use it more effectively than other tools to drive a nail into a wood plank. The second hammer might be marginally helpful as a backup, but is less useful than the first hammer. A third hammer offers little additional benefit. The high value of the first hammer, the lower value of the second hammer and the miniscule value of the third hammer is an example of diminishing marginal returns in which each additional hammer has less value, ceteris paribus.

Hence, diminishing marginal returns yields less productivity (Demirguc-Kunt & Levine, 2009). Imagine that calculators are equally distributed throughout a country, so that each person has a calculator. Now imagine an unequal distribution in which some of the calculators are moved from poorer people to richer people, so that poor people have no calculators and richer people have multiple calculators (e.g., one at home and one at the office). When a calculator is moved from a poor person to a rich person, its productivity falls as its benefit to the rich person (who already has a calculator) is smaller than its benefit to the poor person. Hence, unequal distributions of calculators (or other educational resources) can result in inefficient allocation of resources at the societal level, which reduces productivity (specifically student learning in the realm of education).

INEQUALITIES, MICRO-ECONOMIC MECHANISMS AND ACADEMIC ACHIEVEMENT

These micro-economic mechanisms of rent-seeking behavior and diminishing marginal returns explain how family and school inequalities reduce students' academic achievement (Chiu, 2015). These inequalities reduce educational resources via rent-seeking or reduce resource allocation efficiency via diminishing marginal returns, both of which result in students' lower academic achievement.

Fewer Educational Resources

Family and school inequalities reduce students' academic achievement via rent-seeking at both the national and school levels. In countries with substantial family income inequality, privileged parents often have many more educational resources (e.g., books) at home than others and send their children to private schools (Rothstein, 2000). Hence, they have a strong economic incentive to engage in rent-seeking behavior –paying for lobbyists or personally lobbying politicians or government officials to reduce spending on public schools (e.g., Benabou, 2000). Likewise, in unequal school systems, richer schools may lobby government officials for more educational resources for their schools –and fewer educational resources to other schools (e.g., the Pennsylvania Association of Private School Administrators spent $190,000 on lobbyists during 2008-2012 [Center for Responsive Politics, 2012]). For example, private school officials typically favor educational vouchers for their schools over spending on public schools (e.g., Miller, 1992). Such rent-seeking behavior diverts education resources to lobbying and can reduce national spending on public school resources, resulting in fewer educational opportunities, less learning and lower academic achievement (Chiu & Khoo, 2005).

Parents' rent-seeking behavior within schools can also reduce overall education resources. For example, some parents lobby teachers and principals to cater to the academic needs of their children, sometimes at the expense of other children (Chiu, 2009). Not only is this lobbying unfair, it also takes away teacher time from instruction, which harms all of the students in her classes. In short, rent-seeking at both the national and school levels can reduce educational resources (whether educational materials or teacher time), which can reduce educational opportunities and student learning.

Inefficient Allocation of Resources

Family and school inequalities can also reduce student achievement through unequal distribution of resources, which results in diminishing marginal returns and inefficient resource allocation (Stiglitz, 2012). In a country with substantial family inequality, richer students have many more calculators and other educational resources than poorer students do. As noted above, the values of additional calculators are typically lower, ceteris paribus, so a richer student typically benefits less from an extra book than a poorer student does (Demirguc-Kunt & Levine, 2009). Given a fixed amount of educational resources, distributing them less equally across families (or across schools) within a country allocates these resources inefficiently and magnifies the impact of diminishing marginal returns. Students are likely to learn more overall when all students have one calculator than when some students have multiple calculators and others have none. Hence, when educational resources are less equally distributed, they have less educational value for students on average, who then learn less overall and show lower academic achievement (Chiu, 2015).

Rent-seeking can also exacerbate inefficient allocation of resources and diminishing marginal returns to further reduce overall academic achievement. Privileged parents can ask their children's school principal to assign their child to a course with a better teacher (Lloyd & Blanc, 1996) or ask for more attention to their children's needs. As privileged children often learn the social norms of classrooms at home and have greater cultural capital to create greater affinity with teachers (Bourdieu, 1993), many middle-class teachers already have higher expectations of these privileged students and often give them more attention and assistance (Roscigno & Ainsworth-Darnell's *cultural gatekeeping*, 1999). Hence, lobbying for extra attention for privileged children diverts more teacher time to them rather than less privileged children and result in diminishing marginal returns of teacher time.

CONCLUSION

In short, high SES families have more human capital, financial capital, cultural capital and social capital, and they use them to give their children more learning opportunities, on which the latter often capitalize to learn more. Furthermore, students in higher SES families often attend schools with more resources. Specifically, such schools have better teachers, educational materials and schoolmates, all of which help students learn. Students in these high SES families can often obtain a larger share of school or country resources to aid their own learning. However, these inequalities tend to reduce both overall educational resources and efficiency of resource allocation. When students have fewer educational resources, they have fewer learning opportunities and learn less overall. Also, when resources are inefficiently allocated to richer students who do not need them as much as poorer students, overall student achievement is lower.

REFERENCES

Antikainen, A., & Luukkainen, A. (2008). *Twenty- five years of educational reform initiatives in Finland.* Finland: University of Joensuu.

Banerjee, A., Mookherjee, D., Munshi, K., & Ray, D. (2001). Inequality, control rights and rent seeking: Sugar cooperatives in Maharashtra. *Journal of Political Economy, 109*, 1, 138-190.

Benabou, R. (2000). Unequal societies: income distribution and the social contract. *American Economic Review, 90*, 96-129.

Bourdieu, P. (1993). *The field of cultural production.* New York: Columbia University Press.

Center for Responsive Politics [CRP] (2012). *Influence and lobbying*. Retrieved from http://www.opensecrets.org/lobby/clientsum.php?id=D000055140&year=2012.

Chiu, M. M. (2009). Inequalities' harmful effects on both disadvantaged and privileged students: Sources, mechanisms, and strategies. *Journal of Education Research, 3*, 109-128.

Chiu, M. M. (2010). Inequality, family, school, and mathematics achievement. *Social Forces, 88,* 4, 1645-1676.

Chiu, M. M. (2013a). Class inequality –Achievement. In J. Ainsworth & G. J. Golson's (Eds.), *Sociology of Education* (pp. 116-118). Thousand Oaks, CA: Sage.

Chiu, M. M. (2013b). Family structure and education. In J. Ainsworth & G. J. Golson's (Eds.), *Sociology of Education* (pp. 271-275). Thousand Oaks, CA: Sage.

Chiu, M. M. (2013c). Parental Involvement. In J. Ainsworth & G. J. Golson's (Eds.), *Sociology of Education* (pp. 570-572). Thousand Oaks, CA: Sage.

Chiu, M. M. (2015). Family inequality, school inequalities and mathematics achievement in 65 countries: Microeconomic mechanisms of rent seeking and diminishing marginal returns. *Teacher's College Record, 117,* 1, 1-32.

Chiu, M. M., & Chow, B. W.-Y. (2010). Culture, motivation, and reading achievement. *Learning and Individual Differences*, *20*, 579-592.

Chiu, M. M., & Chow, B. W.-Y. (2015a). International comparisons of student achievement. In S. Rosa's (Ed.), *Progress in Education, vol. 32* (pp. 93-108). Hauppauge, NY: Nova Science.

Chiu, M. M., & Chow, B. W. Y. (2015b). Classmate characteristics and student achievement in 33 countries: Classmates' past achievement, family SES, educational resources and attitudes toward reading. *Journal of Educational Psychology, 107,* 1, 152-169.

Chiu, M. M., & Joh, S. W. (2015). Cross-national comparisons in education-PISA. In James D. Wright (Ed.), *International Encyclopedia of Social and Behavioral Sciences. 2nd Edition, Vol. 5* (pp. 342-348). Oxford: Elsevier.

Chiu, M. M., & Khoo, L. (2003). Rudeness and status effects during group problem solving: Do they bias evaluations and reduce the likelihood of correct solutions? *Journal of Educational Psychology, 95*, 506-523.

Chiu, M. M., & Khoo, L. (2005). Effects of resources, inequality, and privilege bias on achievement. *American Educational Research Journal, 42*, 575-603.

Chiu, M. M., & McBride-Chang, C. (2006). Gender, context, and reading: A comparison of students in 43 countries. *Scientific Studies of Reading, 10*(4), 331-362.

Central Intelligence Agency [CIA]. (2012). *The world factbook*. Washington, DC: CIA.

Cohen, E. G. (1994). Restructuring the classroom: conditions for productive small groups. *Review of Educational Research, 64*(1), 1-35.

Darling-Hammond, L., & Post, L. (2000). Inequality in teaching and schooling: Supporting high quality teaching and leadership in low income schools. In Kahlenberg, R. D. (Ed.), *A notion at risk: preserving public education as an engine for social mobility* (pp. 127-168). New York: The Century Foundation Press.

Demirguc-Kunt, A., & Levine, R. (2009). *Finance and inequality: Theory and evidence* (No. w15275). National Bureau of Economic Research.

Fuller, B., & Clarke, P. (1994). Raising school effects while ignoring culture? Local conditions and the influence of classroom tools, rules, and pedagogy. *Review of Educational Research, 64*, 119-157.

Gamoran, A., & Long, D. A. (2006). Equality of educational opportunity: A 40 year perspective. In R. Teese, S. Lamb, & M. Duru-Bellat (Eds.), *Education and equity: International perspectives on theory and policy* (pp. 3-27). New York: Springer.

Hallinan, M., & Kubitschek, W. (1999). Curriculum differentiation and high school achievement. *Social Psychology of Education, 3*, 41-62.

Hani. (2005, March 7). Illegal donation of 120 million won by high school seniors. *Han Kyu Rae*. Retrieved from http://www.hani.co.kr.

Hanushek, E. A., & Wöbmann, L. (2006). Does educational tracking affect performance and inequality? Differences-in-differences evidence across countries. *The Economic Journal, 116,* C63-C76.

House, R. J., Hanges, P. J., Javidan, M., Dorfman, P. W., & Gupta, V. (Eds.). (2004). *Culture, leadership, and organizations: The GLOBE study of 62 societies.* Thousand Oaks, CA: Sage.

Hoxby, C. M. (2000). Does competition among public schools benefit students and taxpayers?. *American Economic Review, 90*, 5, 1209-1238.

Ilzetzki, E. (2011). Rent-seeking distortions and fiscal procyclicality. *Journal of Developmental Economics, 96,* 1, 30-46.

Lareau, A. (2001). *Unequal childhoods: Class, race and family life*. Berkeley, CA: University of California.

Lloyd, C. B., & Blanc, A. K. (1996). Children's schooling in sub-Saharan Africa: The role of fathers, mothers, and others. *Population and Development Review, 22*(2), 265-298.

Ma, X., & Willms, J. D. (2004). School disciplinary climate: Characteristics and effects on eight grade achievement. *Alberta Journal of Educational Research, 50*(2), 169-188.

Mankiw, N. G. (2004). *Principles of economics* (3rd ed.). Cincinnati: South-Western College.

McKenzie, D. (2005). Measuring inequality with asset indicators. *Journal of Population Economics, 18*, 229-260.

Merryman, J. H., & Perez-Perdomo, R. (2007). *The civil law tradition: An introduction to the legal systems of Europe and Latin America*. Stanford, CA: Stanford University Press.

Miller, J. A. (1992). Private school groups postpone quest for vouchers. *Education Week, 11*, 30, 15.

Murphy, K. M., Shleifer, A., & Vishny, R. W. (1993). Why is rent-seeking so costly to growth? *The American Economic Review, 83*, 2, 409-414.

Oakes, J. (1985). *Keeping track: How schools structure inequality*. New Haven, CT: Yale University Press.

Oakes, J. (1990). *Multiplying inequalities: The effects of race, social class, and tracking on opportunities to learn mathematics and science*. Santa Monica, CA: RAND.

OECD. (2009). *OECD statistics*. Paris: OECD.

Opdenakker, M. C., & Van Damme, J. (2001). Relationship between school composition and characteristics of school process and their effect on mathematic achievement. *British Educational Research Journal, 27*, 407-432.

Pritchett, L. (2001). Where has all the education gone? *The World Bank Economic Review, 15*(3), 367-391.

Rao, P. S., Manohar, P., & Mellam, A. C. (2008). Impact of cultural dimensions on e-learning under face-to-face learning mode and distance learning mode in Papua New Guinea. In H. R. Arabnia's (Ed.), *Proceedings of the 2008 world congress in computer science, computer engineering and applied computing* (pp. 1-6). Athen, GA: University of Georgia.

Rivkin, S., Hanushek, E., & Cain, J. (2005). Teachers, schools and academic achievement. *Econometrica, 73*(2), 417-458.

Roscigno, V. J., & Ainsworth-Darnell, J. W. (1999). Race, cultural capital and educational resources. *Sociology of Education, 72*(3), 158-178.

Rothstein, R. (2000). Equalizing education resources on behalf of disadvantaged children. In R. D. Kahlenberg (Ed.), *A notion at risk* (pp. 127-168). New York: Century.

Rowan, B., Correnti, R., & Miller, R. J. (2002). What large-scale survey research tells us about teacher effects on student achievement: Insights from the prospects study of elementary schools. *Teachers College Record, 104*, 1525–1567.

Samuelson, P., & Nordhaus, W. (2009). *Microeconomics.* New York: Mcgraw-Hill.

Schenk, A., & Oldman, O. (2007). *Value added tax: A comparative approach.* Cambridge: Cambridge University Press.

Schubert, S. R. (2006). Revisiting the oil curse. *Development, 49*, 64-70.

Sirin, S. R. (2005), Socioeconomic status and academic achievement: A meta-analytic review of research. *Review of Educational Research, 75*, 417-53.

Stiglitz, J. E. (2012). *The price of inequality: How today's divided society endangers our future*. New York: Norton.

Sukhtankar, S. (2012). Sweetening the deal? Political connections and sugar mills in India. *American Economic Journal: Applied Economics, 4*(3), 43-63.

United Nations Educational, Scientific and Cultural Organization [UNESCO]. (2010). *Papua New Guinea Country Report*. Paris: UNESCO.

United Nations Children's Fund [UNICEF]. (2011). *The state of the world's children 2001*. Retrieved from http://www.unicef.org/sowc11/

Van Houtte, M. (2004). Tracking effects on school achievement: A quantitative explanation in terms of the academic culture of school staff. *American Journal of Education, 110*, 354-388.

Williams, J. (2005). *Cheating our kids: How politics and greed ruin education*. NY: Palgrave Macmillan.

Willms, D. J., & Somer, M.-A. (2001). Family, classroom, and school effects on children's educational outcomes in Latin America. *School Effectiveness & School Improvement, 12*, 409-445.

BIOGRAPHICAL SKETCH

Name: Ming Ming CHIU
Affiliation: Purdue University
Education:

Ph. D., **University of California, Berkeley**, 1996
Education, Mathematics, Science and Technology
Ed. M., **Harvard University**, Interactive Technology, 1990
B. S., **Columbia University**, Computer Science, *magna cum laude*, 1988

Address:
5156 Beering Hall
Purdue University
100 North Street, West Lafayette, IN, 47907

Research and Professional Experience:
Charles R. Hicks Professor of Educational Psychology and Research Methodology,
2014 – present
Dept of Educational Studies, Purdue University

Professor, Learning and Instruction 2008-2014
University at Buffalo, State University of New York

Associate Professor, Educational Psychology, 2002-2008;
Assistant Professor, 1998-2002
The Chinese University of Hong Kong

Honors:
Outstanding Faculty Discovery Award, Purdue University, Educational Studies, 2015
Top 50 Learning Sciences ideas: Statistical Discourse Analysis (SDA) International Society of the Learning Sciences, 2013
Young Researcher, Chinese University of Hong Kong, 2005
Outstanding Teaching, Chinese University of Hong Kong
Faculty of Education, 1999, 2004, 2007
Leadership Award, Southwest Center, 1996 (US)

Publications Last 3 Years:

Book Chapters (36)

1. Chiu, M. M. (accepted). Statistical discourse analysis. In K. Peppler (Ed.) *SAGE Encyclopedia of Out-of-School Learning*. Thousand Oaks, CA: Sage.
2. Chiu, M. M. (accepted). Social metacognition and knowledge creation in groups. In N. Gotsiridze-Columbus's (Ed.) *Knowledge Creation: New Research.* Hauppauge, NY. Nova Science.
3. Chiu, M. M. (accepted). Chinese families. In Jenifer Kunz's (Ed.) *Family and Parent Leadership*. Thousand Oaks, CA: Sage.
4. Chiu, M. M. (accepted). Self-concept, self-efficacy and mathematics achievement: Students in 65 regions including the US and Asia. In J. Son, J. J. Lo, & T. Watanabe's (Eds.) *What matters? Research trends in international comparative studies in mathematics education in six countries*. New York: Springer.
5. Chiu, M. M. (accepted). Achievement tests. In J. Steinberg (Ed.) *Encyclopedia of Economics and Society*. Thousand Oaks, CA: Sage.
6. Chiu, M. M. (accepted). Asian-American families. In Jenifer Kunz's (Ed.) *Family and Parent Leadership*. Thousand Oaks, CA: Sage.
7. Chiu, M. M. (accepted). Socioeconomic status, inequality and academic achievement. In N. Gotsiridze-Columbus's (Ed.) *Socioeconomic Status: Influences, Disparities and Current Issues.* Hauppauge, NY. Nova Science.
8. Chiu, M. M. (accepted). Early childhood investments. In J. Steinberg (Ed.) *Encyclopedia of Economics and Society*. 4th edition. Thousand Oaks, CA: Sage.
9. Chen, G., & Chiu, M. M. (accepted). Discussion processes in online forums. In M. Khosrow-Pour's (Ed.) *Encyclopedia of Information Science and Technology* (pp. 2544-2554). Hershey, PA: IGI Global.
10. Chiu, M. M. (2015). Statistical discourse analysis. In L. Resnick, C. Asterhan & S. Clarke's (Eds.) *Socializing Intelligence through Academic Talk and Dialogue* (pp. 301-314). Washington, DC: American Educational Research Association [AERA].
11. Chiu, M. M., & Joh, S. W. (2015). Cross-national comparisons in education-PISA. In James D. Wright (Ed.) *International Encyclopedia of Social and Behavioral Sciences. 2nd Edition, Vol. 5* (pp. 342-348). Oxford: Elsevier.

12. Chiu, M. M., & Chow, B. W.-Y. (2015). International comparisons of student achievement. In S. Rosa's (Ed.) *Progress in Education, vol. 32* (pp. 93-108). Hauppauge, NY: Nova Science.
13. Arya, P., Christ, T., & Chiu, M. M. (2015). TAP (**T**eacher learning, **A**pplication to **P**edagogy) through video mediated discussions. In M. L. Niess & H. Gillow-Wiles's (Eds.) *Handbook of Research on Teacher Education in the Digital Age* (pp. 334-356). Hershey, PA: IGI Global.
14. Christ, T., Arya, P., & Chiu, M. M. (2015). A three-pronged approach to video reflection: Preparing literacy teachers of the future. In E. Ortlieb, L. Shanahan, & M. McVee (Eds.), *Video Reflection in Literacy Teacher Education and Development: Lessons from Research and Practice* (pp. 235-253). Bingley, UK: Emerald.
15. Chiu, M. M. (2014). Family and school influences on students' math achievement: United States vs. China. In W. Ma's (Ed.) *East Meets West in Teacher Preparation: Crossing Chinese and American borders* (pp. 143-158). New York: Teachers College Press.
16. Chiu, M. M., & Fujita, N. (2014). Statistical discourse analysis of online discussions: Informal cognition, social metacognition and knowledge creation. In S.-C. Tan, H.-J. So & J. Yeo's (Eds.) *Knowledge creation in education* (pp. 97-112). New York: Springer.
17. Chen, G., & Chiu, M. M. (2014). Learning processes during online discussions. In M. Khosrow-Pour's (Ed.) *Encyclopedia of Information Science and Technology* (pp. 2544-2554). Hershey, PA: IGI Global.
18. Chiu, M. M., & Chen, G. (2014). Collectivism. In L. Ganong, M. Coleman, & G. J. Golson's (Eds.) *The Social History of the American Family* (pp. 254-256). Thousand Oaks, CA: Sage.
19. Chiu, M. M., & Chen, G. (2014). Individualism. In L. Ganong, M. Coleman, & G. J. Golson's (Eds.) *The Social History of the American Family* (pp. 721-724). Thousand Oaks, CA: Sage.
20. Chiu, M. M., & Pawlikowski, M. (2014). Head Start. In L. Ganong, M. Coleman, & G. J. Golson's (Eds.) *The Social History of the American Family* (pp. 660-662). Thousand Oaks, CA: Sage.
21. Chiu, M. M. (2013). Statistical discourse analysis of an online discussion: Cognition and social metacognition. In *Productive Multivocality in the Analysis of Collaborative Learning* (pp. 417-434). New York: Springer.
22. Chiu, M. M. (2013). Classroom interactions between students. In J. Ainsworth & G. J. Golson's (Eds.) *Sociology of Education* (pp. 125-127). Thousand Oaks, CA: Sage.

23. Chiu, M. M. (2013). Social metacognition, micro-creativity and justifications: Statistical discourse analysis of a mathematics classroom conversation. In *Productive Multivocality in the Analysis of Collaborative Learning* (pp. 141-160). New York: Springer.
24. Chiu, M. M. (2013). Class inequality –Achievement. In J. Ainsworth & G. J. Golson's (Eds.) *Sociology of Education* (pp. 116-118). Thousand Oaks, CA: Sage.
25. Chiu, M. M., & Chen, G. (2013). Statistical discourse analysis: Testing hypotheses with large datasets of electronic discourse. In H. L. Lim and F. Sudweeks's (Eds.) *Innovative Methods and Technologies for Electronic Discourse Analysis* (pp. 285-303). Hershey, PA: IGI Global.
26. Chiu, M. M., & * Pawlikowski, M. J. (2013). Social metacognition and micro-creativity. In E. G. Carayannis's (Ed.), *Encyclopedia of Creativity, Invention, Innovation, and Entrepreneurship* (pp. 1687-1692). New York: Springer.
27. Chiu, M. M., * Molenaar, I. Chen, G., Wise, A. F. & Fujita, N. (2013). Micro-analysis of collaborative processes that facilitate productive online discussions: Statistical discourse analyses of three cases. In M. Clara & E. B. Gregori (Eds.) *Assessment and evaluation of time factors in online teaching and learning* (pp. 232-263). Hershey, PA: IGI Global.
28. Chiu, M. M., & Chow, B. W.-Y. (2013). International comparisons of student achievement. In M. Gowda and A. Khanderia's (Ed.) *Educational Achievement: Teaching Strategies, Psychological Factors and Economic Impact* (pp. 115-132). Hauppauge, NY: Nova Science.
29. Chiu, M. M. (2013). Parental Involvement. In J. Ainsworth & G. J. Golson's (Eds.) *Sociology of Education* (pp. 570-572). Thousand Oaks, CA: Sage.
30. Chiu, M. M., * Jones, K. A., & * Jones, J. L. (2013). Building on Schoenfeld's studies of metacognitive control towards social metacognitive control. In Y. Li & J. Moschkovich's (Eds.) *Mathematical proficiency and beliefs in learning and teaching– learning from Alan Schoenfeld and Günter Toerner* (pp. 69-88). Rotterdam, Netherlands: Sense.
31. Chiu, M. M. (2013). Family structure and education. In J. Ainsworth & G. J. Golson's (Eds.) *Sociology of Education* (pp. 271-275). Thousand Oaks, CA: Sage.
32. Chiu, M. M. (2013). Grandparents' role in education. In J. Ainsworth & G. J. Golson's (Eds.) *Sociology of Education* (pp. 333-334). Thousand Oaks, CA: Sage.

33. Chiu, M. M. (2013). Adolescence. In J. Ainsworth & G. J. Golson's (Eds.) *Sociology of Education* (pp. 9-10). Thousand Oaks, CA: Sage.
34. Chiu, M. M. (2013). China. In J. Ainsworth & G. J. Golson's (Eds.) *Sociology of Education* (pp. 114-116). Thousand Oaks, CA: Sage.
35. Wise, A. F., Zhao, Y., Hausknecht, S., & Chiu, M. M. (2013). Temporal considerations in analyzing and designing for online discussions in education: Examining duration, sequence, pace and salience. In M. Clara & E. B. Gregori (Eds.) *Assessment and evaluation of time factors in online teaching and learning* (pp. 198-231). Hershey, PA: IGI Global.
36. Chiu, M. M. (2013). Hong Kong. In J. Ainsworth & G. J. Golson's (Eds.) *Sociology of Education* (pp. 365-366). Thousand Oaks, CA: Sage.

Refereed Journal Articles (27)

1. Chiu, M. M., & Roberts, C. A. (accepted). Improved analyses of single cases: Dynamic multilevel analysis. *Developmental Neurorehabilitation.*
2. Chiu, M. M., & Huang, X. (accepted). Statistical discourse analysis: Students' group problem solving. *Journal of Global Education.*
3. Reynolds, R., & Chiu, M. M. (accepted). Reducing digital divide effects through student engagement in coordinated game design, online resource uses, and social computing activities in school. *Journal of the American Society for Information and Technology.*
4. Lehmann-Willenbrock, N., Chiu, M. M., Lei, Z., & Kauffeld, S. (accepted). Understanding positivity within dynamic team interactions: A statistical discourse analysis. *Group Organization and Management.*
5. Bruce, D., Miller, S. M., & Chiu, M. M. (accepted). Rural students composing videos despite contextual constraints: Breaking down the in-school/out-of school divide. *Learning Media and Technology.*
6. Waight, N., Chiu, M. M., & * Whitford, M. M. (2014). Factors that influence science teachers' selection and usage of technologies in high school science classrooms. *Journal of Science Education and Technology, 23,* 5, 668-681.
7. Chiu, M. M., Chow, B. W. Y., McBride, C., & Mol, S. T. (2016). Students' sense of belonging at school in 41 countries: Cross-cultural variability. *Journal of Cross-cultural Psychology, 47*, 175-196.
8. Chiu, M. M. (2015). Family inequality, school inequalities and mathematics achievement in 65 countries: Microeconomic mechanisms of rent seeking and diminishing marginal returns. *Teacher's College Record, 117,* 1, 1-32.

9. Chiu, M. M., & Chow, B. W. Y. (2015). Classmate characteristics and student achievement in 33 countries: Classmates' past achievement, family SES, educational resources and attitudes toward reading. *Journal of Educational Psychology, 107,* 1, 152-169.
10. Hayden, H. E., & Chiu, M. M. (2015). Reflective teaching via a problem exploration-teaching adaptations-resolution cycle: A mixed methods study of pre-service teachers' reflective notes. *Journal of Mixed Methods Research, 9,* 2, *133-153.* doi:10.1177/1558689813509027
11. Bruce, D. L., & Chiu, M. M. (2015). Composing with new technology: Teachers reflecting on learning digital video *Journal of Teacher Education, 66,* 3, 272-287.
12. Cho, J. R., & Chiu, M. M. (2015). Rapid naming in relation to reading and writing in Korean (Hangul), Chinese (Hanja), and English among Korean children: A one-year longitudinal study. *Journal of Research in Reading, 38,* 4, 387-404.
13. Christ, T., Chiu, M. M., & Wang, X. C. (2015). Emergent readers' social interaction styles and their comprehension processes during buddy reading. *Literacy Research and Instruction, 54*, 1, 45-66.
14. Arya, P., Christ, T., & Chiu, M. M. (2015). Links between characteristics of collaborative peer video analysis events and literacy teachers' outcomes. *Journal of Technology and Teacher Education, 23*(2), 159-183.
15. Chiu, M. M., & Fujita, N. (2014). Statistical Discourse Analysis: A method for modelling online discussion processes. *Journal of Learning Analytics, 1* (3), 61–83.
16. Chiu, M. M., Joh, S. W., & Khoo, L. (2014). Effects of competition and exit threats on managerial incentives in the financial industry. *Review of Financial Information Studies, 3*, 71-89.
17. Molenaar, I., & Chiu, M. M. (2014). Dissecting sequences of regulation and cognition: Statistical discourse analysis of primary school children's collaborative learning. *Metacognition and Learning, 9*, 137-160.
18. Wise, A. F., & Chiu, M. M. (2014). The impact of rotating summarizing roles in online discussions: Effects on learners' listening behaviors during and subsequent to role assignment. *Computers in Human Behavior, 38,* 261-271.
19. Christ, T., Chiu, M. M., & Wang, X. C. (2014). Preschoolers' engagement with reading behaviours: A statistical discourse analysis of peer buddy-reading interactions. *Journal of Research in Reading*, *37*, 4, 375-408.

20. Eryilmaz, E., Chiu, M. M., Thoms, B., Mary, J., & R. Kim. (2014). Design and evaluation of instructor-based and peer-oriented attention guidance functionalities in an open source anchored discussion system, *Computers & Education*, *71*, 303-321. doi: 10.1016/j.compedu.2013.08.009.
21. Christ, T., Arya, P., & Chiu, M. M. (2014). Teachers' reports of learning and application to pedagogy based on engagement in collaborative peer video analysis. *Teaching Education, 25,* 4, 349-374.
22. Arya, P., Christ, T., & Chiu, M. M. (2014). Facilitation and teacher behaviors: An analysis of literacy teachers' video-case discussions. *Journal of Teacher Education, 65* (2), 111-127.
23. Christ, T., Chiu, M. M., * Currie, A., & Cipielewski, J. (2014). The relation between test formats and kindergarteners' expressions of vocabulary knowledge. *Reading Psychology, 35,* 6, 499-528.
24. Reynolds, R., & Chiu, M. M. (2013). Formal vs. informal context factors as contributors to student engagement in a guided discovery-based program of game design learning. *Learning, Media and Technology, 38,* 4, 429-462.
25. Hayden, H. E., & Chiu, M. M. (2013). Lessons learned: Supporting the development of reflective practice and adaptive expertise. *Literacy Research Association Yearbook, 62*, 278-296.
26. Wang, X. C., Christ, T., & Chiu, M. (2013). Exploring a comprehensive model for early childhood vocabulary instruction: A design experiment. *Early Childhood Development and Care, 187*(7), 1075-1106. DOI: 10.1080/03004430.2013.843531
27. Moore-Russo, D., * Viglietti, J. M., Chiu, M. M., & * Bateman, S.M. (2013). Teachers' spatial literacy as visualizing, reasoning, and communication. *Teaching and Teacher Education, 29*, 97-109.

In: Socioeconomic Status
Editor: Geoffrey Perkins

ISBN: 978-1-63485-326-2

Chapter 2

SOCIOECONOMIC STATUS AND EXECUTIVE FUNCTIONS IN CHILDREN: IMPLICATIONS FOR A SCHOOL-BASED COGNITIVE INTERVENTION

Vanessa Arán-Filippetti [*] ***and María Cristina Richaud***
Interdisciplinary Center of Mathematical and Experimental Psychology Research "Dr. Horacio J. A. Rimoldi" (CIIPME). National Scientific and Technical Research Council (CONICET), Argentina

ABSTRACT

In recent years, within the scope of neuroscience, a marked increase in research in the field of cognitive development associated with Socioeconomic Status (SES) has been evidenced, with specific emphasis on the analysis of cognitive-executive processes. The present chapter reviewed literature on socioeconomic variables that predict the child's executive functioning and possible contextual and cognitive variables mediating this association. It is concluded that low-SES children would not demonstrate a primary dysexecutive deficit, but rather a difficulty in performing executive tasks effectively, due to a lack of specific stimulation for the development of these functions. It is expected that the integration of these contributions will ease both the understanding of the nature of the dysexecutive profile associated with SES, and the design of

[*] Corresponding Author: Email: vanessaaranf@gmail.com.

intervention strategies to integrate the educational endeavor. Early stimulation becomes then instrumental in reversing the negative effect of environmental poverty on children's cognitive and socioemotional development.

Keywords: socioeconomic status, executive functions, cognitive intervention, children

INTRODUCTION

1. Executive Functions and Socioeconomic Status

In recent years, within the scope of neuroscience, the knowledge about cognitive development associated with SES has increased significantly, with a particular emphasis on the study of executive processes. Executive Functions (EF) is a term that encompasses a series of cognitive processes such as (a) working memory, (b) inhibition and (c) cognitive flexibility (Miyake et al., 2000), needed to perform goal-oriented behaviors (Luria, 1966; Stuss & Benson, 1986). These functions are associated with prefrontal cortex (PFC) activity and reciprocal interconnections with other cortical areas and subcortical structures (Fuster, 1997; Heyder, Suchan, & Daum, 2004).

There are different reasons underlying the growing interest in the study of executive functioning associated with SES, among which the following are worthy to mention: 1) studies with experimental animal models have proved that the PFC development is sensitive to a vast range of factors in the prenatal (Fride & Weinstock, 1988), perinatal, and postnatal (Sullivan & Brake, 2003) stages; 2) the PFC and the EF follow a course of postnatal development (Diamond, 2002; Fuster, 2002), enabling early daily life experiences to influence these brain regions; and 3) brain imaging studies have found an association between SES and patterns of frontal lobe brain activity (Kishiyama, Boyce, Jimenez, Perry, & Knight, 2009; Otero, Pliego-Rivero, Fernández, & Ricardo, 2003; Tomarken, Dichter, Garber, & Simien, 2004). There has been further evidence obtained through behavioral studies that have consistently demonstrated the existence of differential cognitive executive profiles among low-SES children and middle-SES children (Arán Filippetti, 2011; Arán Filippetti & Richaud de Minzi, 2011; Farah et al., 2006; Noble, Norman, & Farah, 2005; Noble, McCandliss, & Farah, 2007). Thus, although there are data on the existence of a disexecutive cognitive profile associated with SES, there is no still strong evidence indicating which socioeconomic variables play a more important role in the prediction of executive task performance and the possible mediators of these associations.

The present chapter firstly analyzes evidence from brain and behavioral studies as regards neurocognitive profiles associated with SES; it later reviews that research examining the socioeconomic variables that predict the executive performance and possible cognitive variables mediating this association. We consider that these theoretical and empirical developments offer understanding of the nature of the dysexecutive profile associated with SES, laying the foundation for the implementation of actions that may favor the child's development. Understanding those specific factors that influence children's cognitive development and the mechanisms through which they act, clearly enables to delimit specific actions to strengthen the child's cognitive functioning. Hence, it is expected that the integration of these contributions will ease the articulation between research in neuroscience and the intervention in the educational and family field, favoring the design of intervention strategies in terms of the cognitive processes sensitive to SES.

2. Brain Studies and SES

2.1. Electrophysiological Recordings

Different studies conducted with electroencephalographic (EEG) records and brain evoked potentials (BEPs) have demonstrated an association between SES and brain activity in children and adolescents.

Among these works, an important number were carried out in Mexico by Otero and his group (Otero 1994, 1997; Otero et al., 2003) who analyzed patterns of brain development through EEG records in children of different ages: 18 to 30 months of age; 4 years old and 5 to 6 years old. They found a delay in both the maturation of the right temporal areas at the age of 4 (Otero, 1997) and the left temporal areas at the age of 6. According to the authors, differences in the temporal regions are due to lower verbal stimulation experienced by children at risk and a delay in the start of schooling. Furthermore, they found a delay in the maturation of the frontal regions that persists at 5 and 6 years old. In these studies, it was concluded that inadequate or insufficient environmental stimulation is the factor that most significantly contributes to the delay in brain maturation evidenced in low-SES children.

In another study conducted with 12 to 14 years-old adolescents, Tomarken et al., (2004) found that SES predicts left frontal brain activity. The authors suggest that this association would be mediated by chronic stress and other environmental factors associated with SES, such as maternal warmth, social support, instability among peer groups, and cognitive stimulation.

Kishiyama et al., (2009) conducted a study with electrophysiological recordings in children of 7-12 years old in order to analyze the association between SES and the underlying neuronal activity in the prefrontal region; they found a reduced prefrontal activity in low-SES children during attention tasks. According to the authors, these results confirm those of previous behavioral studies that suggest that social inequality is associated with impaired prefrontal function in low-SES children. In turn, they state that a number of factors related to child rearing may have contributed to these results, such as higher levels of stress and lack of access to cognitively stimulating material and learning experiences during development.

Finally, by means of BEPs, distinct studies have shown differences according to SES in patterns of neural responses during selective attention tasks (D'Angiulli, Stapells, Hertzman, & Herdman, 2008; Stevens, Lauinger, & Neville, 2009).

2.2. Magnetic Resonance Imaging (MRI)

One of the pioneering studies in using functional MRI in order to understand the relationship between brain activity and behavior was that of Noble, Wolmetz, Ochs, Farah, and McCandliss (2006). The former work evaluated 6 to 9 year-old children from different SES, equate in terms of the level of phonological awareness, and proved that SES modulates the relationship between the brain activity in the left fusiform gyrus and perisylvian regions and phonological language skills.

Meanwhile, Raizada, Richards, Meltzoff, and Kuhl (2008) investigated the relationship among SES, functional brain activity and a battery of cognitive and linguistic test in 5 years-old children and found that SES is strongly associated with the degree of hemispheric specialization in the left inferior frontal gyrus, evidenced by less brain activation during behavioral rhythmic tasks. The authors concluded that lower language skills associated with SES are related to a lower underlying neural specialization, and the differences would be explained by factors associated with SES, as the parental education level and the language to which the child is exposed.

More recently, Jednoróg et al., (2012) analyzed the relationship between SES and brain structure in 23 healthy children aged 10 years, and found that low SES is associated with minor gray matter volumes in the bilateral hippocampi, the middle temporal gyri, the left fusiform and the right inferior occipito-temporal gyri.

Another study in this line is that of Sheridan, Sarsour, Jutte, D'Esposito, and Boyce (2012) who found an association between parental SES and the prefrontal cortex (PFC) function in children aged 8-12 years. The authors also found that the possible mechanisms through which the SES impacts on PFC function would be the level of language used at home and stress reactivity.

These brain imaging studies provide important evidence about brain processes underlying the behavioral differences observed in different studies. Unfortunately, few works have used these techniques in the study of cognitive differences associated with SES.

3. Behavioural Studies on SES and EF

As previously mentioned, the study of those executive processes associated with SES has significantly increased in recent years. Its importance lies in the fact that enables both to identify the sensitivity of different cognitive sub-processes related to school learning and to design intervention strategies for working with low-SES children.

According to Hughes and Ensor (2009) there are three lines of evidence that point towards an association between the EF and the social environment: 1. Although studies in adult twins have shown that dementia has a strong genetic influence, they in turn stress the importance of the social influence at the onset of the disease and the course of cognitive decline. 2. Genetic factors frequently interact with environmental influences: genetic vulnerability is expressed upon exposure to environmental stressors such as abuse or family chaos and 3. Intervention studies show an increase in the performance of EF pointing to the influence of the environment on these functions.

A significant group of researchers that examine the cognitive functions associated with SES suggest analyzing the cognitive profiles in terms of neurocognitive systems and their association with underlying brain areas (Farah et al., 2006; Noble et al., 2005, 2007). According to the authors, the importance of this analysis lies in the fact that the possibility to evaluate different neurocognitive systems allows inferring the most sensitive cognitive functions to SES and further intervening on those aspects most affected. One of their first studies reports significant differences by SES as regards the perisylvian language and the executive/prefrontal systems (Noble et al., 2005). In a subsequent study, Farah et al., (2006) found significant differences according to SES in the area of language, verbal memory, working memory and cognitive control, but no differences in visual and rewards proccessing tasks. In their most recent study, Noble et al., (2007) deepened the analysis of the executive system by identifying three subsystems within the construct: working memory, cognitive control system and reward processes. Results indicate significant differences in the working memory and cognitive control executive-systems, and in the language and the parietal system. Overall, these studies invariably show the same results and reach similar conclusions: the perisylvian/language system, the medial temporal/memory system, the lateral prefrontal/working memory and the anterior cingulate/cognitive control system become the neurocognitive systems most sensitive to SES. However, studies do not account for a deficiency in the ventromedial-prefrontal/reward system. The authors conclude that the ventromedial system would be less sensitive to SES in relation to the prefrontal system as ventromedial regions mature earlier than other brain regions (Farah et al., 2006).

In Latin American countries there also exists a growing interest in the study of executive processes associated with SES.

Thus, for instance, in a study conducted with 622 children from Colombia and Mexico, it was found an influence of the parents' educational level and type of school on the development of EF (Ardila, Rosselli, Matute, & Guajardo, 2005). In Argentina, Lipina, Martelli, Vuelta, Injoque-Ricle, and Colombo (2004) carried out a work in which the executive performance of 247 school children aged 3 to 5 years with unsatisfied basic needs (UBN) and satisfied basic needs (SBN) were compared. A battery of tests was administered to measure different executive domains. According to the results, children with UBN would have a less efficient performance as regards cognitive flexibility, the achievement of objectives and attentional control. In a later study, Lipina, Martelli, Vuelta, and Colombo (2005) analyzed the performance on the A-not-B executive task in 6-14 months-old infants with different basic needs. In this study, it was found that children with UBN give less correct answers and make a greater number of perseverative and non-perseverative errors than the group of children with SBN.

In turn, Musso (2010) found an association between poverty and the performance obtained by children in processes such as problem solving, planning and cognitive control. Besides, the author found that the child's perception of hostile parental control becomes a significant predictor of planning ability.

Consistent with previous research, more recent studies also conducted with Argentine children have found that children from low SES demonstrate a lower cognitive performance in tasks that assess EF regarding children of middle SES (see e.g., Arán Filippetti & Richaud de Minzi, 2011; Arán Filippetti & Richaud de Minzi, 2012). It is worthy to note that while the performance of low-SES children is lower than that of middle-SES children, both the factor structure of the EF and the development of these cognitive processes are similar in both groups (Arán Filippetti, 2013). This suggests that the observable cognitive profile in low-SES children would be mainly due to inexperience rather than a permanent deficit in the mechanisms necessary for the development of these functions, for there is a gradual increase of these functions with age but not a stable deficit in development (Arán Filippetti, 2011; Arán Filippetti, 2013).

Overall, the various studies suggest an association between SES and executive functioning, which would be independent of the child's mother tongue and their home country.

4. Predictive and Mediating Factors of Cognitive Performance Associated with SES

Previous research has examined those possible causal mechanisms and mediating variables that would explain the lower executive functioning associated with SES. These studies become a significant contribution to understand the effects of SES on brain function, enabling the design of educational policies and intervention programs that address the most influential variables and mechanisms by which socioeconomic indicators may act.

In general, there is consensus among studies indicating that socioeconomic indicators have different effects on cognitive functions. For instance, in the study by Noble et al., (2007), the influence of SES -measured according to the educational level, parental occupational level and family income-, and the performance on different cognitive functions such as language, memory, and the EF system were analyzed. Results firstly showed an association between SES and the performance in every variable evaluated, except for the reward system. Furthermore, when analyzing possible mediating factors of this association, they found that: (1) the school environment accounts for variations in language performance, verbal memory, and working memory, and (2) in terms of literacy, the home environment explains part of the variance in the performance of working memory. Besides, they found that by controlling language, the association between SES and cognitive control was removed and reduced in terms of visuospatial skills, memory and working memory; thus, they suggest that language would be the cognitive variable mediating this association. Finally, the authors found that the association between SES and the evaluated functions increased after removing the sample of children with medical and psychiatric history, showing that those factors related to health factors would not mediate the association between SES and cognitive function.

In a subsequent study, Farah et al., (2008) analyzed the relationship among the performance on the language and memory systems and environmental stimulation, parental nurturance, maternal intelligence and substances abuse in prenatal stage. The authors concluded that: (1) the environmental stimulation at home explains variations in language, and (2) parental upbringing patterns explain the performance in tasks that demand working memory.

Meanwhile, Sarsour et al., (2011) analyzed the association between family SES and single parenthood and the EF - inhibitory control, cognitive flexibility, and working memory- as well as those potential mediating and moderating variables of this association. The authors found that family SES predicted the performance on all the EF analyzed, and that low-SES children who were living with a single parent showed a lower performance than those low-SES children who were living with two parents. Besides, the authors found that parental responsivity, enrichment actions, and family companionship mediate the association between SES and the performance in working memory and inhibitory control tasks.

More recently, Hackman, Gallop, Evans, and Farah (2015) found that family income and maternal education predict first graders planning ability, while household income predicts working memory at 54 months of age. The early childhood maternal sensitivity would mediate the relationship between maternal education and planning, whereas early childhood home characteristics would mediate the association between SES and EF. The authors also found that this association between SES and EF remained across early and middle childhood.

Table 1. SES and Executive Functions

Authors	SES Indicators /mediators	Task	Age	Main Results
Arán Filippetti, & Richaud de Minzi (2011)	*SES indicator*: • Type of school	• Matching Familiar Figures Test–20 • WPPSI mazes	6 years old	SES is associated with the reflexivity-impulsivity cognitive style and planning ability
Arán Filippetti, & Richaud de Minzi (2012)	*SES indicator*: • Family income • MEL • Occupational level • HC *Mediating factors*: • IQ • Cognitive impulsivity	• Kaufman Brief Intelligence Test • Matching Familiar Figures Test–20 • Stroop Color-Word Interference Test • Wisconsin Card Sorting Test • Digit span and letter-number sequencing subtests of the WISC IV • Porteus Maze • Controlled Oral Word Association Test	7-12 years old	MEL and HC predict EF task performance Cognitive impulsivitybut not IQ levels mediates the relationship between SES and EF
Ardila et al., (2005)	*SES indicator*: • Parents' educational level	• Matrices • Similarities • Graph and verbal fluency • Card Sorting • Pyramid of Mexico	5-14 years old	Parental education level is associated with children performance on EF tasks
Lipina et al., (2004)	*SES indicator*: • NES scale	• A-not-B task • Spatial Reversal • Color Reversal • Three and Four Colors • Strrop-like Day-Nigth • Tower of London	3-5 years old	UBN Children had a lower performance in most of the executive tasks analized
Lipina et al., (2005)	*SES indicator*: • NES scale	A-not-B task	6-14 months old	UBN Children make a higher number of mistakes as regards children with SBN
Noble et al., (2005)	*SES indicator*: • Hollingshead index *Mediating factors*: • Child's language	Battery of tasks that assess five broad neurocognitive systems: visual cognition, visuospatial processing, memory, language and EF	5 years old	Low SES children get a lower performance on measures that value the left perisylvian/language system and the prefrontal/ executive system Laguage ability mediate mediate the association between SES and EF

Table 1. (Continued)

Authors	SES Indicators /mediators	Task	Age	Main Results
Farah et al., (2006)	*SES indicator*: • Hollingshead index	Battery of tasks designed to assess seven key neurocognitive systems: Lateral PFC/ Working memory, Anterior cingulate cortex/Cognitive control system, Ventromedial PFC/Reward processing system, Occipitotemporal/ Pattern vision system, Parietal/Spatial cognition system, Medial temporal/ Memory system, and Left perisylvian/ Language system	10-13 years old	SES has a main effect on the perisylvian/language and Medial temporal/ Memory systems, and a minor one on the Lateral/Prefrontal/Working memory and Anterior cingulate/Cognitive Control systems
Noble et al., (2007)	*SES indicator*: • Education • Ocupation • Family income *Mediating factors*: • Child's health • Child's language • Home environment • School environment	Battery of tasks that assess six broad neurocognitive systems: language, visuospatial processing, memory, working memory, cognitive control, and reward processing	6 years old	SES account for variance in language, working memory and cognitive control Language ability and environmental factors mediate the association between SES and EF
Musso (2010)	*SES indicator*: • Type of school	• Simon says • Tower of Hanoi	6-10 years old	Children at risk for poverty showed a lower performance on problem solving and cognitive control tasks
Sarsour et al., (2011)	*SES indicator*: • The MacArthur Research Network on SES and Health Questionnaire *Mediating factors*: • HOME inventory	• Digit span subtest from the WISC III • Trail Making Test (Trails A and B) • Stroop Test	8-12 years old	Family SES is associated with the child EF task performance. Enrichment activities, Parental responsivity, and family companionship mediate the relationship between SES and the EF of working memory and inhibitory control

In various studies conducted with Spanish-speaking children, we have also analyzed those socioeconomic indicators that predict cognitive executive task performance and the possible mediating variables of this association. Regarding predictive indicators, we found that from the different socioeconomic variables analyzed (i.e., occupational status, maternal educational level, family income and housing conditions), only the maternal educational level (MEL) and housing conditions (HC) significantly predict performance on tasks that assess language, attention (Arán Filippetti, 2012), and EF (Arán Filippetti & Richaud de Minzi, 2012). As regards possible mediating variables, we found that in line with that found by Noble et al., (2007), language partially mediates the association between SES and cognitive performance. Besides, we found that cognitive impulsivity, but not the level of IQ, mediates the relationship between SES and the performance on tasks that value EF. Thus, the level of intelligence would not determine the differences found in the executive functioning, but rather these differences could be partly explained by a greater cognitive impulsivity (Arán Filippetti & Richaud de Minzi, 2012).

Overall, the reviewed studies suggest that the relationship between SES and children's cognitive performance would be explained by specific socioeconomic variables and by various factors -related also to the child's social context- that would mediate or moderate such association. Apparently, the different socioeconomic indicators would have dissociable effects on EF and there would be a greater influence of some factors over others, such as parental educational level In Table 1 we summarize some of the major studies examining the relationship between SES and EF.

CONCLUSION

Several studies have found a lower cognitive performance associated with SES in the area of intellectual abilities (McLoyd., 1998; Bradley & Corwyn 2000; Brooks-Gunn & Duncan, 1997), the language and the level of vocabulary reached (Hoff 2003; Hoff & Tian, 2005) and the performance on tasks that assess attention and memory (Arán Filippetti, 2012; Matute, Sanz, Gumá, Rosselli, & Ardila, 2009). However, the current emphasis within the field of cognitive neuroscience would be primarily placed on the analysis of those EF associated with the PFC areas of the brain since this is the brain area following the latest ontogeny development of the neocortex and consequently, it is hypothesized that it would be more sensitive to experience during postnatal development. In this line, studies conducted with both English-speaking children (see e.g., Farah et al., 2006; Mezzacappa, 2004; Noble et al., 2005, Noble et al., 2007) and Spanish-speaking children (see e.g., Arán Filippetti, 2011; Arán Filippetti, 2013; Arán Filippetti & Richaud de Minzi, 2012; Ardila et al., 2005; Lipina et al., 2004; Lipina et al., 2005; Musso, 2010) have demonstrated consistently that low-SES children get lower cognitive performance in various tasks that measure executive functioning compared to middle-SES children.

Among those socioeconomic factors that would explain this lower executive performance associated with SES, the studies reviewed stress the parental education level, the parental occupational level and housing conditions. However, apparently, the association between SES and the cognitive executive performance would be mainly due to the parental education level (see, e.g., Arán Filippetti & Richaud, 2012; Ardila et al., 2005, Noble et al., 2005; Noble et al., 2007). This suggests that there would be a pre-eminent influence of the environment over a deficit of an organic base, enabling to reconsider the dysexecutive profile associated to SES as a difficulty to perform executive tasks due to the lack of specific stimulation for the development of these functions.

Another significant line of research favoring the hypothesis of the environmental influence on cognitive development, comes from studies and intervention programs carried out with low-SES students. Through its implementation, it has been demonstrated that there is a possibility to increase the cognitive performance after interventions which are not so prolonged. These programs include: *The Abecedarian Program* (Ramey & Campbell, 1991; Campbell et al., 2008; Barnett & Masse, 2007), *The Perry Preschool Program* (Weikart, 1998; Belfield, Nores, Barnett, & Schweinhart, 2006) and *The Child-Parent Center* (CPC) Program (Reynolds & Temple, 1998; Reynolds, Temple, Robertson, & Mann, 2001; Reynolds et al., 2007) among others. Meanwhile, Diamond, Barnett, Thomas, and Munro (2007) used an intervention program based on Vygotsky's theory, in a population of low-SES preschool children named *Tools of the Mind* (Bodrova & Leong, 2007). Results of this program showed that self-regulation and EF may be increased with exercise. Barnett et al., (2008) also found an improvement in executive performance after the implementation of Tools of the Mind in children aged 3-4 years, but lower increments regarding language development. Moreover, in Argentina, within the framework of the research project "Resilience development in children under environmental risk due to extreme poverty"[1], there have been several studies that show an improvement in executive task performance in low-SES children through a systematic training at schools settings (Arán Filippetti & Richaud de Minzi, 2011; Ghiglione, Arán Filippetti, Manucci, & Apaz, 2011; Richaud & Arán Filippetti, 2015).

Finally, a recent study provides further evidence for the hypothesis of a dysexecutive profile secondary to the SES effect (Arán Filippetti & Richaud, 2012) when proving that the socioeconomic variables –MEL and HC– directly influence the executive performance and indirectly act through cognitive impulsivity. In this regard, it becomes significant the vast empirical evidence indicating that cognitive impulsivity is susceptible to change and that reflective disposition can be trained. Hence, if this is one of the mechanisms through which the SES causes a lower executive performance, this could be reverted.

Although it may be argue that neurofunctional differences have been found by means of neuroimaging studies in low-SES children, which would further imply a deficit of organic origin, we consider that such deficit would be also a secondary one, as a result of the lack of environmental stimulation during postnatal development. Previous studies have concluded that the differences found in brain activity as measured by EEG records in low-SES children are mainly due to economic disadvantages and the low maternal education level (Harmony, Marosi, Diaz de Leon, Becker, & Fernandez, 1990) as well as the lack of environmental stimulation (Otero et al., 2003).

Thus, it would be not appropriate to define the cognitive differences associated with SES in terms of an "executive deficit" since, although the empirical evidence points to a low executive task performance, distinct studies have consistently argued that differences in the cognitive area should be the effect of the environment that would act across multiple mediating processes rather than primary organic causes. In this regard, Raizada and Kishiyama (2010) state that neuroscience studies that analyze the cognitive performance in low-SES children must overcome the concept of "deficit" and propose just the opposite, actually establishing firm guidelines in order to optimize educational opportunities for these children.

At this point, the contributions of Vigotsky's theory deserve to be resumed, for they stress the importance of social interaction in the appropriation of knowledge by the child and the role of private speech on self-

[1] Research project conducted by María Cristina Richaud de Minzi, Ph.D., and financed by the *Ministerio de Ciencia, Tecnología e Innovación Productiva* (PICT 03/14064, FONCYT 2005-2007).

regulation of behavior. In this sense, both the school and the family represent the child closest contexts through which different actions that may positively affect their executive functioning can be implemented.

Specifically in schools settings, intervention programs should focus on stimulating the executive abilities jointly with the teaching of school skills, promoting the effective use of executive strategies both at the moment of assimilating new contents, and when trying to remind or express what has already been learned (Arán Filippetti & Lopez, 2014). As specific strategies, it becomes effective to use those that favor and promote children's self regulation. Examples include the *Self-instructional training* of Meichenbaum and Goodman (1971), cognitive modeling and/or programs based on the teaching of steps for problem solving, among others. It is also important for the teacher to recognize and describe those areas of EF difficulty for the child in order to plan the correct stimulation and carry out and register clear changes. During class work at the beginning of each activity, it is effective that the teacher indicates the steps to take so as to achieve the tasks objectives, monitor the child's performance while doing the task, paying attention to the necessary steps for its implementation, evaluate the whole process and encourage the child to both check his/her performance and their self-correction. This supervision should be gradually removed, for the child to achieve internal control over his/her behavior. In turn, within the family scope, and considering that these functions follow a course of postnatal development, parents can also foster the emergence of executive processes, favoring their development. Research in this area has shown that parental support and guidance to the child while performing goal-oriented tasks, favors the development of EF (Hughes & Ensor, 2009).

In summary, there exist various studies showing that: (a) there is a significant association between SES and the child executive performance (Arán Filippetti & Richaud de Minzi, 2011; Arán Filippetti & Richaud de Minzi, 2012; Farah et al., 2006; Lipina et al., 2004; Noble et al., 2005; Noble et al., 2007) and (b) the parental education level would be the main predictor (see e.g., Arán Filippetti & Richaud de Minzi, 2012; Noble et al., 2005). This suggests that differences in the cognitive area would be mainly due to environmental factors. Conclusions of several studies (Kishiyama et al., 2009; Otero et al., 2003; Tomarken et al., 2004) add to the former hypothesis, indicating by means of neuroimaging techniques, that brain differences associated with SES are mainly due to the lower cognitive stimulation, parental characteristics, and environmental stress.

We consider that the study of these brain self-regulatory functions becomes of particular interest in the design of educational policies aimed at reducing the impact of SES on cognitive performance, for it has been proved in previous research that those interventions that act on self-regulation, self-control and the EFs are more beneficial for low-SES children as they have extended long-term effects on academic performance. According to Raizada and Kishiyama (2010), a particular interesting aspect in the training of the EF are the long-term positive effects, since an increase in self-control clearly eases attention, helping the child to experience learning situations in a meaningful way and thus assisting intellectual growth.

REFERENCES

Arán Filippetti, V. & López, M. B. (2014). *The role of executive functions in academic competences: an analytical review*, (pp. 305–322). En Bennett, K. P. (Ed.). *Executive functioning. Role in early learning processes, impairments in neurological disorders and impact of cognitive behavior therapy*. New York: Nova Science Publishers, Inc.

Arán Filippetti, V. (2011). Funciones ejecutivas en niños escolarizados: efectos de la edad y del estrato socioeconómico. *Avances en Psicología Latinoamericana*, *29*, 98-113.

Arán Filippetti, V. & Richaud de Minzi, M. C. (2011). Efectos de un programa de intervención para aumentar la reflexividad y la planificación en un ámbito escolar de alto riesgo por pobreza. *Universitas Psychologica*, *10*, 341-354.

Aran Filippetti, V. & Richaud de Minzi, M. C. (2012). A structural analysis of executive functions and socioeconomic status in school-age children: cognitive factors as effect mediators. *The Journal of Genetic Psychology*, *173*, 393-416.

Arán Filippetti, V. (2012). Estrato socioeconómico y habilidades cognitivas en niños escolarizados: Variables predictoras y mediadoras. *Psykhe*, *21*, 3-20.

Arán Filippetti, V. (2013). Structure and invariance of executive functioning tasks across socioeconomic status: Evidence from spanish-speaking children. *The Spanish Journal of Psychology*, *16*, 1-15.

Ardila, A., Rosselli, M., Matute, E. & Guajardo, S. (2005). The influence of the parents educational level on the development of executive functions. *Developmental Neuropsychology*, *28*, 539-560.

Barnett, W. & Masse, L. (2007). Comparative benefit-cost analysis of the Abecedarian program and its policy implications. *Economics of Education Review*, *26*, 113-125.

Barnett, W. S., Jung, K., Yarosz, D. J., Thomas, J., Hornbeck, A., Stechuk, R., et al., (2008). Educational effects of the tools of the mind curriculum: A randomized trial. Early *Childhood Research Quarterly*, *23*, 299-313.

Belfield, C., Nores, M., Barnett, S. & Schweinhart, L. (2006). The High/Scope Perry Preschool Program: Cost benefit analysis using data from the age-40 follow-up. *The Journal of Human Resources*, *XLI*, 162-190.

Bodrova, E. & Leong, D. J. (2007). *Tools of the mind: The Vygotskian approach to early childhood education* (2nd ed, pp. 341-354). Upper Saddle River, N.J.: Prentice-Hall.

Bradley, R. H. & Corwyn, R. F. (2002). Socioeconomic status and child development, *Annual Review of Psychology*, *53*, 371-399.

Brooks-Gunn, J. & Duncan, G. J. (1997). The effects of poverty in children. The Future of Children. *Children and Poverty*, *7*(2) – Summer/Fall.

Campbell, F. A., Wasik, B., Pungello, E. P., Burchinal, M. R., Barbarin, O. A., Kainz, K., Sparling, J. & Ramey, C. T. (2008). Young adult outcomes of the Abecedarian and care early childhood educational interventions. *Early Childhood Research Quarterly*, *23*, 452-466.

D'Angiulli, A., Herdman, A., Stapells, D. & Hertzman, C. (2008). Children's event-related potentials of auditory selective attention vary with their socioeconomic status. *Neuropsychology*, *22*(3), 293-300.

Diamond, A. (2002). Normal development of prefrontal cortex from birth to young adulthood: Cognitive functions, anatomy, and biochemistry. In D. T. Stuss & R. T. Knight (Eds.), *Principles of frontal lobe function* (pp. 466–503). London: Oxford University Press.

Diamond, A., Barnett, W. S., Thomas, J. & Munro, S. (2007). Preschool program improves cognitive control. *Science*, *318*, 1387-1388.

Farah, M., Shera, D., Savage, J., Betancourt, L., Giannetta, J., Brodsky, N., Malmud, E. & Hurt, H. (2006). Childhood poverty: Specific associations with neurocognitive development. *Brain research*, *1110*, 166-174.

Farah, M. J., Betancourt, L., Shera, D. M., Savage, J. H., Giannetta, J. M., Brodsky, N. L., Malmud, E. K. & Hurt, H. (2008). Environmental stimulation, parental nurturance and cognitive development in humans. *Developmental Science*, *11*, 793-801.

Fride, E. & Weinstock, M. (1988). Prenatal stress increases anxiety related behavior and alters cerebral lateralization of dopamine activity. *Life Sciences*, *42*, 1059-1065.

Fuster, J. M. (1997). *The Prefrontal Cortex: Anatomy, Physiology, and Neuropsychology of the Frontal Lobe. 3rd edn.* Philadelphia: Lippincott-Raven.

Fuster, J. M. (2002). Frontal lobe and cognitive development. *Journal of Neurocytology*, *31*, 373-385.

Ghiglione, M. E., Arán Filippetti, V., Manucci, V. & Apaz, A. (2011). Programa de intervención, para fortalecer funciones cognitivas y lingüísticas, adaptado al currículo escolar en niños en riesgo por pobreza. *Interdisciplinaria*, *28*, 17-36.

Hackman, D. A., Gallop, R., Evans, G. W. & Farah, M. J. (2015). Socioeconomic status and executive function: developmental trajectories and mediation. *Developmental science*, *18*, 686-702.

Harmony, T., Marosi, E., de León, A. E. D., Becker, J. & Fernández, T. (1990). Effect of sex, psychosocial disadvantages and biological risk factors on EEG maturation. *Electroencephalography and clinical Neurophysiology*, *75*, 482-491.

Heyder, K., Suchan, B. & Daum, I. (2004). Cortico-subcortical contributions to executive control. *Acta Psychologica*, *115*, 271-289.

Hoff, E. (2003). The specificity of environmental influence: socioeconomic status affects early vocabulary development via maternal speech. *Child Development*, *74*, 1368-1378.

Hoff, E. & Tian, C. (2005). Socioeconomic status and cultural influences on language. *Journal of Communication Disorders*, *38*, 271-278.

Hughes, C. H. & Ensor, R. A. (2009). How do families help or hinder the emergence of early executive function? In C. Lewis & J. I. M. Carpendale (Eds.), *New Directions in Child and Adolescent Psychiatry*, 123, 35-50.

Jednoróg, K., Altarelli, I., Monzalvo, K., Fluss, J., Dubois, J., Billard, C. & Ramus, F. (2012). The influence of socioeconomic status on children's brain structure. *PloS one*, *7*(8), e42486.

Kishiyama, M. M., Boyce, W., Jimenez, A. M., Perry, L. M. & Knight, R. T. (2009). Socioeconomic Disparities Affect Prefrontal Function in Children. *Journal of cognitive neuroscience*, *21*, 1106-1115.

Lipina, S. J., Martelli, M. I., Vuelta, B. L., Injoque-Ricle, I. & Colombo, J. A. (2004). Pobreza y desempeño ejecutivo en alumnos preescolares de la ciudad de Buenos Aires (Republica Argentina). *Interdisciplinaria*, *21*, 153-193.

Lipina, S. J., Martelli, M. I., Vuelta, B. & Colombo, J. A. (2005). Performance on the A-not-B task of Argentinean infants from unsatisfied and satisfied basic needs homes. *Revista interamericana de psicología*, *39*, 49-60.

Luria, A. R. (1966). Higher cortical functions in man. New York: Basic Books.

Matute, E., Sanz, A., Gumá, E., Rosselli, M. & Ardila, A. (2009). Influencia del nivel educativo de los padres, el tipo de escuela y el sexo en el desarrollo de la atención y la memoria. *Revista Latinoamericana de Psicología*, *41*, 257-276.

McLoyd, V. C. (1998). Socioeconomic disadvantage and child development. *American Psychologist*, *53*, 185–204.

Meichenbaum, D. H. & Goodman, J. (1971). Training impulsive children to talk to themselves: A means of developing self-control. *Journal of Abnormal Psychology*, *77*, 115-126.

Mezzacappa, E. (2004). Alerting, orienting, and executive attention: Developmental properties and sociodemographic correlates in an epidemiological sample of young, urban children. *Child Development*, *75*, 1373-1386.

Miyake, A., Friedman, N. P., Emerson, M. J., Witzki, A. H., Howerter, A. & Wager, T. D. (2000). The unity and diversity of executive functions and their contributions to complex "Frontal Lobe" tasks: A latent variable analysis. *Cognitive Psychology*, *41*, 49-100.

Musso, M. (2010). Funciones ejecutivas: un estudio de los efectos de la pobreza sobre el desempeño ejecutivo. *Interdisciplinaria*, *27*, 95-110.

Noble, K. G., Norman, M. F. & Farah, M. J. (2005). Neurocognitive correlates of socioeconomic status in kindergarten children. *Developmental Science*, *8*, 74-87.

Noble, K. G., Wolmetz, M. E., Ochs, L. G., Farah, M. J. & McCandliss, B. D. (2006). Brain-behavior relationships in reading acquisition are modulated by socioeconomic factors. *Developmental Science*, *9*, 642–654.

Noble, K. G., McCandliss, B. D. & Farah, M. J. (2007). Socioeconomic gradients predict individual differences in neurocognitive abilities. *Developmental Science*, *10*, 464–480.

Otero G. (1994). EEG spectral analysis in children with sociocultural handicaps. *International Journal of Neuroscience*, *79*, 213-220.

Otero, G. A. (1997). Poverty, cultural disadvantage and brain development: a study of pre-school children in Mexico. *Electroencephalography and Clinical Neurophysiology*, *102*, 512–516.

Otero, G. A., Pliego-Rivero, F. B., Fernandez, T. & Ricardo, J. (2003). EEG development in children with sociocultural disadvantages: a follow-up study. *Clinical neurophysiology*, *114*, 1918-1925.

Raizada, R. D. S., Richards, T. L., Meltzoff, A. N. & Kuhl, P. K. (2008). Socioeconomic status predicts hemispheric specialisation of the left inferior frontal gyrus in young children. *Neuroimage*, *40*, 1392–1401.

Raizada, R. D. S. & Kishiyama, M. M. (2010). Effects of socioeconomic status on brain development, and how cognitive neuroscience may contribute to levelling the playing field. *Frontiers in human neuroscience*, *4*, 1-11.

Ramey, C. T. & Campbell, F. A. (1991). Poverty, early childhood education, and academic competence: The Abecedarian experience. In A. C. Huston (Ed.), *Children reared in poverty: Child development and public policy* (pp. 190-221). New York: Cambridge University Press.

Reynolds, A. J. & Temple, J. A. (1998). Extended early childhood intervention and school achievement: Age thirteen findings from the Chicago Longitudinal Study. *Child Development*, *69*, 231-246.

Reynolds, A. J., Temple, J. A., Ou, S. R., Robertson, D. L., Mersky, J. P., Topitzes, J. W. & Niles, M. D. (2007). Effects of a school-based, early childhood intervention on adult health and well-being: A 19-year follow-up of low-income families. *Archives of Pediatric Adolescent Medicine*, *161*, 730-739.

Reynolds, A. J., Temple, J. A., Robertson, D. L. & Mann, E. A. (2001). Long-term effects of an early childhood intervention on educational achievement and juvenile arrest: A 15-year follow-up of low-income children in public schools. *JAMA: Journal of the American Medical Association*, *285*, 2339-2346.

Richaud, M. C. & Arán Filippetti, V. (2015). Children's Cognitive Development in Social Vulnerability: An Interventional Experience. *Psychology Research*, *5*, 684-692.

Sarsour, K., Sheridan, M., Jutte, D., Nuru-Jeter, A., Hinshaw, S. & Boyce, W. T. (2011). Family socioeconomic status and child executive functions: the roles of language, home environment, and single parenthood. *Journal of the International Neuropsychological Society*, *17*, 120-132.

Sheridan, M. A., Sarsour, K., Jutte, D., D'Esposito, M. & Boyce, W. T. (2012). The impact of social disparity on prefrontal function in childhood. *PLoS One*, *7*, e35744.

Stevens, C., Lauinger, B. & Neville, H. (2009). Differences in the neural mechanisms of selective attention in children from different socioeconomic backgrounds: An event-related brain potential study. *Developmental Science*, *12*, 634–646.

Stuss, D. T. & Benson, D. F. (1986). *The frontal lobes*. New York: Raven Press.

Sullivan, R. M. & Brake, W. G. (2003). What the rodent prefrontal cortex can teach us about attention-deficit/hyperactivity disorder: the critical role of early developmental events on prefrontal function. *Behavioural Brain Research*, *146*, 43–55.

Tomarken, A. J., Dichter, G. S., Garber, J. & Simien, C. (2004). Resting frontal brain activity: linkages to maternal depression and socio-economic status among adolescents. *Biological Psychology*, *67*, 77–102.

Weikart, D. P. (1998). Changing early childhood development through educational intervention. *Preventive Medicine*, *27*, 233-237.

Biographical Sketches

Name: Vanessa Arán Filippetti

Affiliation: Interdisciplinary Center of Mathematical and Experimental Psychology Research (CIIPME). National Scientific and Technical Research Council (CONICET)

Education: Ph.D. in Psychology

Address: Teniente General Juan Domingo Perón 2158, C1040AAH. Buenos Aires, Argentina

Research and Professional Experience:

- Assistant Researcher, CONICET
- Titular Professor, *Universidad Adventista del Plata*

Publications Last 3 Years:

- Arán Filippetti, V. (2013). Structure and Invariance of Executive Functioning Tasks across Socioeconomic Status: Evidence from Spanish-Speaking Children. *The Spanish Journal of Psychology*, *16*, 1-15.
- Arán Filippetti, V., & López, M. B. (2013). Las funciones ejecutivas en la clínica neuropsicológica infantil. *Psicología desde el Caribe*, *30*, 380-415.
- Arán Filippetti, V., & Krumm, G. L. (2013). Executive Functions and Attention in School-Age Children according to the Behavioral Profile Rated by their Teachers. *International Journal of Psychological Research*, *6*, 101-109.

- Krumm, G. L., Arán Filippetti, V., Lemos, V., Aranguren, M., & Rubilar, J. V. (2013). Invariancia de Medidas de la prueba de figuras del Test de Pensamiento Creativo de Torrance según la edad: Un estudio en niños y adolescentes de habla hispana. *Cuadernos de Neuropsicología*, *7*, 29-49.
- Krumm, G., Lemos, V., & Arán Filippetti, V. (2014). Factor Structure of the Torrance Tests of Creative Thinking Figural Form B in Spanish-Speaking Children: Measurement Invariance across Gender. *Creativity Research Journal*, *26*, 72-81.
- López, M. B, Arán Filippetti, V., & Richaud, M. C. (2014). Empatía: Desde la Percepción Automática hasta los Procesos Controlados. *Avances en Psicología Latinoamericana*, *32*, 37-51.
- Vargas-Rubilar, J., & Arán Filippetti, V. (2014). Importancia de la Parentalidad para el Desarrollo Cognitivo Infantil: una Revisión Teórica. *Revista Latinoamericana de Ciencias Sociales, Niñez y Juventud*, *12*, 171-186.
- Krumm, G. L., Aranguren, M., Arán Filippetti, V., & Lemos, V., (2014). Factor Structure of the Torrance Tests of Creative Thinking Verbal Form B in a Spanish-speaking Population. *The Journal of Creative Behavior*, *0*, 1–15.
- López, M. B., & Arán Filippetti, V. (2014). Consecuencias de la exposición prenatal a alcohol: desarrollo histórico de la investigación y evolución de las recomendaciones. *Revista Colombiana de Obstetricia y Ginecología*. *65*, 162 -173.
- Krumm, G. L., Arán Filippetti, V., & Bustos, D. (2014). Inteligencia y Creatividad: Correlatos entre los Constructos a través de dos Estudios Empíricos. *Universitas Psychologica*, *13*(4).
- Aguer, V., & Arán Filippetti, V. (2014). Funciones ejecutivas en niños escolarizados según el nivel de rendimiento en cálculo. *ACTA psiquiátrica y psicológica de América Latina*, *60*(4), 236-344.
- Arán-Filippetti, V., Krumm, G. L. & Raimondi, W. (2015). Habilidades Intelectuales y sus Correlatos con las Funciones Ejecutivas: Un estudio en Niños y Adolescentes. *Revista Neuropsicología Latinoamericana*, 7, 24 – 33.
- López, M. B., Arán Filippetti, V. & Cremonte, M. (2015). Consumo de alcohol antes y durante la gestación en la Argentina: prevalencia y factores asociados. *Revista Panamericana de Salud Pública/Panamerican Journal of Public Health*, *37*, 211 - 217

- Krumm, G. L., Arán-Filippetti, V., & Aranguren, M. (2015). Creatividad verbal según sexo y edad: Un estudio en adolescentes y jóvenes de habla hispana. *ACTA psiquiátrica y psicológica de América Latina*, *61*, 184-194.
- Arán Filippetti, V. & Richaud, M. C. (2014). Do executive functions predict written composition? Effects beyond age, verbal intelligence and reading comprehension. *Acta Neuropsychologica*, *13*, 331-349.
- Richaud, M. C. & Arán Filippetti, V. (2015). Children's Cognitive Development in Social Vulnerability: An Interventional Experience. *Psychology Research*, *5*, 684-692.
- Arán Filippetti, V. & López, M. B. (2014). The role of executive functions in academic competences: An analytical review. En Bennett, K. P. (Ed.). *Executive functioning. Role in early learning processes, impairments in neurological disorders and impact of cognitive behavior therapy (cbt)* (pp. 305 – 322). ISBN 978-1-63321-194-0.

Name: María Cristina Richaud

Affiliation: Interdisciplinary Centre of Research in Mathematical and Experimental Psychology (CIIPME). National Scientific and Technical Research Council (CONICET)

Education: Ph.D. in Psychology

Address: Tte. Gral. Perón 2158 1040, Buenos Aires, Argentina

Research and Professional Experience: Superior Researcher CONICET; Director of CIIPME

Honors:

- **Bernardo Houssay Award 2005** to the scientific and technological research for the Consolidated Researcher in the Great Area of Human and Social Sciences issued by the Ministry of Science, Technology and Productive Innovation of the Nation. Resolution No. 1291-1205, November 15, 2005.
- **ACIERA Woman Award 2009** to the scientific researcher for her contribution to the solution of psychosocial problems. Legislature of the City of Buenos Aires. March 9, 2009.

- **Rubén Ardila Award for Scientific Research in Psychology 2009**, issued by the Foundation for the Advancement of Psychology to the trajectory, for the research work throughout life through original, creative work, with contributions to psychology as a science.
- **Recipient of 2013 APA Award for Distinguished Contributions to the International Advancement of Psychology** (For her distinguished career as a researcher and educator who has contributed significantly to the growth of psychology as a scientific discipline in Argentina and in Latin America, and for her efforts to internationalize and shape the future of psychology in Argentina, Latin America and beyond). Hawai, Julio de 2013.
- **Award Carlo Molinari Mariotto** of the Association for the Advancement of Psychological Science, for the outstanding contribution to the advancement of scientific psychology in Argentina. November 2014.

Publications Last 3 Years:

- Richaud de Minzi, M. C. (2013). Children perception of parental empathy in relation with children empathy. *The Journal of Psychology: Interdisciplinary and Applied*, *147*(6), 1-14.
- Richaud, M. C., Mestre, M. V., Lemos, V., Samper, P., Ghiglione, M. y Tur, A. (2013). La influencia de la cultura en los estilos parentales en contextos de vulnerabilidad social [The culture influence on parental styles in contexts of social vulnerability]. *Avances de Psicología Latinoamericana*, *31*(2), 419-431.
- Richaud, M. C., Mesurado, B., Samper, P., Llorca, A., Tur, A. y Lemos, V. (2013). Estilos parentales, inestabilidad emocional y agresividad en niños de nivel socioeconómico bajo en Argentina y España [Parental styles, emotional instability, and aggressiveness in low socioeconomic level children in Argentina and Spain]. *Ansiedad y Estrés*, *19*(1), 53-69.
- Richaud, M. C. y Iglesias, F. (2013). Evaluación del afrontamiento en niños pequeños. *Subjetividad y procesos cognitivos*, 17(1), 244-256.
- Richaud, M. C. (Noviembre 2013). Contributions to the study and promotion of resilience in socially vulnerable children. *American Psychologist*, *68*(8), 751-758. doi: 10.1037/a0034327
- Richaud de Minzi, M. C. (2013). Influencia del fortalecimiento de recursos socioemocionales, cognitivos y lingüísticos sobre el

afrontamiento de la amenaza. Un estudio en niños en vulnerabilidad social. *Revista de Peruana de Psicología y Trabajo Social*, *2*(2), 87-96.

- Richaud, M. C. y Bei, E. (2013). Construcción de una escala para evaluar el contexto familiar desde la perspectiva de los padres. *Interdisciplinaria*, *30*(2), 283-296. Q3
- Mestre, M. V., Mesurado, B., Tur, A., Samper García, P y Richaud, M. C. (2014). Adaptación y validación en población española de la Escala de Expectativa de los hijos adolescentes sobre la reacción de sus padres frente al comportamiento prosocial y antisocial. *Universitas Psicológica*, 13(1), 61-70.
- López, M., Arán, V., Richaud de Minzi, M. C. (2014). Empatía: Algunos Debates en torno al Concepto. *Avances de Psicología Latinoamericana*, *32*, 37-51.
- Cupani, M., Pilatti, A., Urrizaga, A., Chincolla, A. y Richaud de Minzi, M. C. (junio de 2014). Inventario de personalidad IPIP-NEO: estudios preliminares de adaptación al español en estudiantes argentinos. *Revista Mexicana de Investigación en Psicología* 6(1), 1-14.
- Mesurado, B., Richaud, M. C., Mestre, M. V., Samper, P., Tur, A., Morales Mesa, S. y Viveros, E. F. (October 2014). Parental expectations and prosocial behavior of adolescents from low-income backgrounds. A cross-cultural comparison between three countries: Argentina, Colombia and Spain. *Journal of Cross-Cultural Psychology*, *45*, 1471-1488. Published online 13 July 2014.DOI: 10.1177/0022022114542284 The online version of this article can be found at: http:// jcc.sagepub.com/ content/ early/ 2014/ 07/12/ 0022022114542284
- Andrés, M. L., Castañeiras, C. E. y Richaud, M. C. (2014). Contribución de las estrategias cognitivas de regulación emocional en la ansiedad, depresión y bienestar en niños de 10 años de edad. Resultados preliminares. *Psiencia*, 6(2), 81-89.
- Andrés, M. L., Castañeiras, C. E., Richaud, M. C. (2014). Relaciones entre la personalidad y el bienestar emocional en niños. El rol de la regulación emocional. *Cuadernos de Neuropsicología– Panamerican Journal of Neuropsychology*, *8*(2), 217-241. DOI: 10.7714/cnps/ 8.2.205

- Richaud, M. C. (2014). Algunos aportes sobre la importancia de la empatía y la prosocialidad en el desarrollo humano. *Revista Mexicana de Investigación en Psicología*, 6(2), 171-176.
- Oros, L. y Richaud de Minzi, M. C. (2015). How to Assess Joy in Childhood. Utility and Functioning of a Picture Scale. Psychology, 6, 223-233. Published Online February 2015 in SciRes. http:// www.scirp.org/ journal/ psychhttp:// dx.doi.org/ 10.4236/ psych. 2015.63022
- Oros, L. B., Menghi, M. S., Richaud de Minzi, M C., Ghiglione, M. E. (2015). Educar en medios socialmente vulnerables. El valor de la capacitación docente. *Contextos educativos: Revista de educación*, 18, 79-92
- Mesurado B., Richaud, M. C., & Niño, N. J. (2015). Engagement, Flow, Self-efficacy and Eustress of University Students: A cross-national comparison between the Philippines and Argentina, *The Journal of Psychology: Interdisciplinary and Applied*, in press.
- Arán Filipetti, V. & Richaud, M. C. (2015). Do Executive Functions Predict Written Composition? Effects beyond Age, Verbal Intelligence and Reading Comprehension. *Acta Neuropsychologica, 13*(4), 331-349.
- Andrés, M. L., Canet, C, Castiñeiras, C., & Richaud, M. C. (2016). Relaciones de la regulación emocional y la personalidad con la ansiedad y depresión en niños. *Avances de Psicología Latinoamericana, 34(1)*, 99-115. Doi: dx.doi.org/ 10.12804/ apl34. 1.2016.07
- Richaud, M.C., & Arán Filippetti, V. (2015). Children´s Cognitive Development in Social Vulnerability: An Interventional Experience. Journal of Psychology Research, 12(5), 684-692 doi:10.17265/2159-5542/2015.12.003
- Samper García, P., Mesurado, B., Richaud, M. C., & Llorca, A. (2016). Estructura Factorial del Cuestionario de Conciencia Emocional adolescentes españoles. Interdisciplinaria, 33(1), in press
- Andrés, M. L., Richaud, M. C., Castañeiras, C. E., Canet-Juric, L. & Rodríguez-Carvajal, R. (2016). Neuroticism and depression in children: the role of cognitive emotional regulation. Journal of Genetic Psychology. In press

Chapters:

- Richaud, M. C., Lemos V. y Vargas Rubilar, J. (2013). Argentine culture and parenting styles. In H. Selin (Ed.), Parenting Across Cultures (pp. 277-292). The Netherlands: Springer Publishers. ISBN 978-94-007-7503-9.
- Mesurado, B. y Richaud, M. C. (2013). Children's Perception of Parental Relationships and Personality Traits in Argentinian Children. In E. E. Crossman & M. A. Weiler (Eds.), Personality Traits: Causes, Conceptions and Consequences (pp.1-26). Hauppauge, NY: Nova Editorial Publishers. ISBN 978-1-62618-398-8. E-book ISBN 978-1-62618-399-5.
- Mesurado, B. y Richaud, M. C. (2013). The relations between the Perceived Parenting Styles and the Neuroticism in Argentinean Children and Adolescents. In K. Parn (Ed.), Psychology and neuroticism (pp.43-66). Hauppauge, NY: Nova Editorial Publishers. ISBN 978-1-62808-150-3.
- Richaud de Minzi, M. C. (2013). Argentine Questionnaire on Coping for Children 8-12 Years of age 26-29; Argentine Scale of Perception of the Relationship with Parents for Children 13-17 Years of age 29-34; Argentine Scale of Perception of the Relationship with Parents for Children 8-12 Years of age 35-39. In P. Orpinas. A. Rico, & L. Martínez (Comp.), Latino Families and Youth: A compendium of assessment tools. Section I: Parent-child communication (pp. 26-39). Washington, D.C.: Pan American Health Organization.
- Mesurado, B., & Richaud, M. C. (2014). Optimal Experience in Argentinean Children and Adolescents. En A. Castro Solano (Ed.), Positive Psychology in Latin America. Chapter 9 (pp.161-179). Springer. ISBN 978-94-017-9034-5.
- Lemos, V., & Richaud, M. C. (2014). Promotion of childhood prosocial behavior in school environment. En A. Castro Solano (Ed.), Positive Psychology in Latin America. Chapter 10 (pp.179-195). Springer. ISBN 978-94-017-9034-5.
- Richaud, M. C., & Lemos, V. (2014). Promotion of resiliency in children in social vulnerability: an approach from positive psychology. En A. Castro Solano (Ed.), Positive Psychology in Latin America. Chapter 11 (pp.195-213). Springer. ISBN 978-94-017-9034-5.

- McGinley, M., Opal, D., Richaud, M. C., & Mesurado, B. (2014). Cross-Cultural Evidence of Multidimensional Prosocial Behaviors: An Examination of the Prosocial Tendencies Measure (PTM). In L. Padilla-Waker & G. Carlo (Eds.), Prosocial Development: A multidimensional approach (pp. 258-278). New York: Oxford University Press. ISBN-10: 0199964777 | ISBN-13: 978-0199964772
- Mesurado, B., Mateo, N. J., Valencia, M. & Richaud, M. C. (2014). Extraversion: Nature, Development and Implications to Psychological Health and Work Life. In A. D. Haddock & A. P. Rutkowski, Psychology of Extraversion (pp.107-120). Hauppauge, NY: Nova.
- Richaud, M. C. (2014). Desarrollo de la empatía y su relación con la prosocialidad. Algunas estrategias de intervención en habilidades sociales y emociones positivas. En V. Mestre, P. Samper y A. Tur-Porcar (coord.), Desarrollo prosocial en las aulas: propuestas para la intervención (pp. 299-315). Valencia: Tirant lo Blanch.
- Musso, M. F., Richaud, M. C., & Cascallar, E. (Julio 2015). Auto-regulación y Funciones Ejecutivas: aportes para comprender el aprendizaje y el desempeño escolar. En I. E. J. Huaire, A. Elgier y G. Maldonado Paz (Comp.), Psicología Cognitiva y Procesos de Aprendizaje. Aportes desde Latinoamérica (pp.25-47). Universidad Nacional de Educación Enrique Guzmán y Valle "Alma Mater del Magisterio Nacional."
- Richaud, M. C., Lemos, V. N. & Oros, L. B. (2016). Empathy in children. Theory and assessment. In D. F. Watt and J. Panksepp, Psychology and neurobiology of Empathy (Chapter 5). Hauppauge, NY: Nova Editorial Publishers, in press. ISBN version impresa: 978-1-63484-446-8. ISBN ebook: 978-1-63484-448-2

In: Socioeconomic Status
Editor: Geoffrey Perkins
ISBN: 978-1-63485-326-2

Chapter 3

SOCIOECONOMIC AND RACIAL DISPARITIES IN CHILD HEALTH OUTCOMES

Crystal N. Piper[1], MPH, MHA, PhD, and Corliss Solomon[2], MPH
Department of Public Health Sciences,
University of North Carolina at Charlotte, Charlotte, NC, US
[1]Assistant Professor, Public Health Sciences
[2]Graduate Research Assistant, Public Health Sciences

ABSTRACT

This chapter will examine socioeconomic and racial disparities in child health and health outcomes. A better understanding of the functions of minority families and how parent's behaviors and characteristics affect children's' health and health outcomes is essential in developing a family-centered approach to child health care. Research suggest that the use of health care services among children is primarily determined by parents and resembles the utilization patterns of parents. These previous studies are of particularly concern as minority families have historically been less likely to seek health care services in a timely manner. A number of social and demographic factors, particularly socioeconomic status can have tremendous impacts on family functioning and child health outcomes. This chapter will examine the literature and explore some of the contemporary social influences that shape minority families impact on child physical health and health behaviors that include: socioeconomic status, family structure, and social support and functioning.

INTRODUCTION

Guidance, support, and affection are just a few of the essential factors impacting the life of a child. Not only are these factors needed but they must be of good quality to be advantageous, as the quality of interactions between a parent and child is essential to optimal child development (Chen, 2014). One area in particular in a child's life in which a family can be influential is health, including health outcomes and health behaviors. Broadly speaking, parenting, family structure, family socioeconomic (income & education) status, and the physical environment all impact health outcomes. For instance, consider the nutrition and physical activity levels of lower income families. The family's income may determine where they live and the health related services they may have access to. In fact, the neighborhood may be in a high crime area, which limits safe play outside for children or they may reside in a food desert, which is the physical environment where affordable and nutritious food is difficult to obtain. All of these familial factors impact the health of the child. This chapter will explore the influence of parenting, family structure, socioeconomic status, race/ethnicity, neighborhood, environment, and interaction with the healthcare system on a child's health outcomes and behaviors.

IMPACT OF PARENTING AND FAMILY STRUCTURE ON CHILD HEALTH

Parenting

A child's overall health outcomes and life experiences is primarily shaped by parenting. More specifically, the impact of parenting on the child can have both negative and positive outcomes. A history of family dysfunction is related to negative parenting behaviors and often passed on from parent to child (Sipsma et al., 2010). On the other hand, satisfaction with the relationship between both parents of the child has been found to be related with more positive parenting behaviors and family outcomes (Rueger et al., 2007). While both women and men are typically a part of the parenting process, women and men often differ in their involvement in a child's life. For example, compared to fathers, mothers are typically more attentive to the needs of the child (Rhoads, 2005).

Family influence on a child's health outcomes is often explained by parenting style. Parenting self-efficacy is associated with positive child socio-emotional adjustment, and different aspects of parenting can affect efficacy. Individuals with low parenting efficacy often have children that are at risk for adverse psychosocial outcomes (Angley et al., 2014). Moreover, family members typically resemble one another in terms of health behaviors both positive and negative. For example, a child's use of health services is largely controlled by their parents and typically resembles the health care utilization patterns of their parents. Parents generally decide for children which symptoms require medical attention or restriction of activities, although they may establish different thresholds for seeking medical care for themselves. Additionally, parental factors are important predictors of children deciding to engage in unhealthy behaviors like smoking (Fleming et al., 2002). Parent influences include the parents own smoking status. The impact of parental factors may be mediated through parental influences, which in turn influence teen attitudes and tobacco use. Many adult smokers have their initial smoking experience as a teenager and Black parents are more likely to smoke than White parents (Skinner et al., 2009). On the other hand, positive health behaviors such as physical activity and nutrition intake can also be dictated by parental influences.

Case Study: Parenting and Pain

Let's take a closer look at the impact of parenting on chronic pain in children. An important consideration in children's health is the bidirectional parent and family influences on pain management in children. Children sometimes experience pain related to injuries, burns, or chronic diseases such as cancer. Parental characteristics such as behaviors and emotions play an important role in children's pain experiences, where overly protective parent behaviors, increased distress, and history of chronic pain are important parent level influences. Families of children with chronic pain have poorer family functioning, more conflict, and less cohesion than families of healthy children (Palermo et al., 2014).

It is well understood that parents of children with chronic pain often have a disrupted and dysfunctional family life. Parents of children with chronic pain report experiencing high levels of parenting stress, anger, depressive symptoms, and anxiety. A lack of communication within the family may lead to poorer pain management for the child. Families of children with chronic pain also experience a financial burden caring for their sick child.

The health status of the parents is also an important factor to consider in the management of chronic pain in children. Maternal poor health and function are associated with poorer health and functioning in children with chronic conditions. Many types of chronic pain conditions cluster in families, and a child with a headache is more likely to have a parent with a headache. It is well understood that parent and family factors may influence the pain experience of children.

Family Structure

While, the parenting of a child is usually performed by the child's biological mother and father, it is not uncommon for a child to be raised in a single parent household. In fact, it is not unusual for the parenting of a child to be done by grandparents or same sex couples. Whatever the case may be, family type has been found to be related to a child's physical and psychosocial wellbeing. Some children have higher risk of poor physical and psychosocial well-being, and the presence of certain second adults in the family structure has important ameliorative functions, such as mother/grandmother families have demonstrated nearly as effective outcomes as mother/father families. The adults that makes up the parental unit for a child, whether old, young, rich or poor can greatly impact health outcomes.

It is well understood that children growing up with two biological married parents have access to greater economic, social, and health care resources. Closer supervision of children in two-parent families appears to be associated with better health outcomes. While a significant number of children live with same-sex parents, it is not clear if the same health benefits are experienced. For example, due to societal stereotypes, children of same-sex parents often face social isolation and often do not access health care in a timely manner, because the parent's fear the child may be ostracized. Moreover, while it is common for children to live in blended families, it has been shown that children in blended families do not fare as well as those living with two biological married parents (Brown, 2004). Nevertheless, young Black children in multigenerational households have better development outcomes compared to Black children who live in single parent homes (Entwisle and Alexander, 1996).

Single parent households have drastically increased over the past four decades. This trend may also be impacted by the increase of divorces, which has resulted in a number of single parent households. In fact, children of divorced parents are at higher risk of emotional and behavior problems, including depression, and poor school performance. Children in single parent families experience a variety of negative consequences, such as behavioral, social, emotional, and academic problems, and in general, White single mothers have a higher economic status than Black single mothers (Foster and Kalil, 2007). Single mothers of African American children are less likely than single mothers of Caucasian children to take their children to the doctor for treatment or prevention (Thompson et al., 2001).

As the numbers of single mothers on governmental assistance programs continue to increase, concerns have been raised about the well-being of their children. Young single mothers are less likely to utilize positive health behaviors such as breastfeeding (Hannon et al., 2000). Additionally, poor single mothers may have low socioeconomic status, low ability, and low psychological functioning. These same variables also could predict poor child health outcomes. A large number of young black children are being raised by a single mother, making this a significant issue across many levels.

In the United States, approximately four million children are being raised by their grandparents. Even though this phenomenon occurs in all racial/ethnic groups it is more prevalent among African Americans families. Historically, Black grandmothers have been an integral part of the family system and have functioned in an interactive role. The increased rates of grandparent caregiving in African American communities may also reflect a long tradition of grandparent involvement in childrearing, rooted in West African traditions, an important symbolic meaning for many of today's African American families. The great migrations north in the first half of the century also contributed to more grandparents caring for grandchildren, when African American children where often left in the care of southern grandparents while their parents sought employment.

Grandparents caring for children are more likely to be female, to have not completed high school, to be younger in age, living in poverty, and faced with many additional costs related to education, health care, and other basic needs of the child in their care (Minkler and Thompson, 2005). For example, children in the care of their grandparents lack access to health insurance (Bryson and Casper, 1999). Black grandparents bear a disproportionate burden of grandparent caregiving for the nation's children. Also important to note is the contemporary African American grandparent caregiving often occurs in response to crisis.

Impact of Family Socioeconomic Status on Child Health

Poverty has been described as an economic state that does not allow for the provision of basic family and child needs. The culture of poverty is in part mediated through environmental deprivations, such as failing schools, gangs, drugs, violence, and struggling families. In the United States 1 in 5 children grow up in poverty and are frequently deprived of a supportive environment to grow and develop (Wood, 2003). The majority of children that are poor are non-Hispanic Blacks. Since the mid to late 1990s, the poverty rate for children under the age of 6 has continued to increase. Families struggle daily that are living at or below the poverty threshold (Edin and Lein, 1997). The percentage of poor families with working adults continues to increase, and many families depend solely on government assistance programs. Due to the continuous rise in childhood poverty rates and increasing single-parent households it is imperative to examine the complex relationships between race, family structure, and children's health.

Family and Child Health Outcomes

Poor health outcomes are associated with minority families that have low socioeconomic status and other social class factors. Family socioeconomic status is the strongest single predictor of diminished health and well-being for children. Socioeconomic status is strongly associated with parental education, which further contributes to the culture of deprivation that children who are poor experience. Poverty is also associated with single parent households. This is true for both Black born and Black immigrant families.

Children who spend a greater proportion of their childhood in poverty are expected to experience diminished health through increased exposure to poor health conditions as well as potentially more dire conditions. Exposure to lead hazards is an example of how a child living poverty and poor conditions directly impacts child health. Children in poor families are five times as likely to be in fair or poor health (5%) as children in families that were not poor as (1%) (Bloom, Jones, and Freeman, 2013).

Families with low social capital are linked to social isolation, which might impact their ability to access resources and health information to make better choices for their children. Moreover, family socioeconomic status is associated with poor nutrition, exposure to worse environmental conditions, reduced access to healthcare, and worse outcomes from disease. Socioeconomic status is also associated with higher rates of chronic health problems and injuries in children. Children from poor families are more likely to be born prematurely or with a low birthweight and have a higher mortality rates throughout childhood (Jackson et al., 2000). Black children are less likely to receive adequate well child care, and access and use of pediatric health services among Blacks continues to be below the national average (El-Mohandes, et al., 2003).

The number of children impacted by poverty is on the rise. The sharp rise in childhood poverty since the mid-1970s is primarily the result of declining socioeconomic status, especially the relative and absolute decline of fathers' income for children in the bottom half of the income distribution, with unemployment and underemployment contributing. All of these factors lead families to delay necessary health care and contribute to poorer health status for all the family members.

Insurance and Access to Care

While publically funded programs like Medicaid provide some assistance, when compared to children with private insurance there are still major disparities. Even though publicly funded programs, such as Medicaid have improved children's access to health insurance, they do not necessarily address access to care and the many other barriers associated with family poverty. In fact, low-income families may experience financial barriers to accessing appropriate and timely health care. These barriers may be attributable to the family's lack of health insurance.

Minority adolescents in impoverished high crime areas typically lack resources that promote positive health behaviors. For African-American children family support has been shown to improve health and dietary compliance. Non-Hispanic Black children and poor children are more likely to have been diagnosed with asthma compared to other racial and income groups (Sidora et al., 2012).

Statistics

- Children with private health insurance are more likely to be in excellent health (64%) than children with Medicaid or other public coverage (48%).
- Children with Medicaid or other public coverage are more likely to have had 2 or more ER visits in the past 12 months (9%) than children with no health insurance (5%) or private health insurance (3%).
- Children with Medicaid (10%) are more likely than children with private health insurance (6%) or children with no health insurance coverage (5%) to have received special education or early intervention services.
- Children in poor families are more likely to use a clinic as their usual place of health care (37%) than children in families that are not poor (16%).
- Approximately 1.2 million children are unable to get needed medical care because the family could not afford it (2%) and medical care for 2.1 million children was delayed because of worry about the cost (3%).
- Uninsured children (10%) are 5 times likely as children with private insurance (2%) or Medicaid coverage (2%) to have not had contact with a doctor or other health professional in more than 2 years.
- Uninsured children are more than 5 times likely to have an unmet dental need (21%) as children with private health insurance (4%).
- Nine percent of children are in families with an income less than 35k and 10% of children are in families with an income of 35-49k had no health insurance, compared with 2% of children in families with an income of 100k or more.
- Black children are more likely to visit the emergency room in the past 12 months, than White (5%) and Asian (1%) children.
- Non-Hispanic White children are more likely to have had a dental visit in the past 6 months (67%) than non-Hispanics Black (63%) and Hispanics (61%). (Bloom, Jones, and Freeman, 2013).

Neighborhood and Environment

Children in poverty face many problems, especially as it relates to their neighborhood and environment. Environment is strongly associated with a child's health status. Families in poverty have a greater disadvantage in maternal resources and are more likely to reside in neighborhoods of concentrated poverty and experience more exposure to health risks (Malat, Oh, and Hamilton, 2005). Many poor children reside in older homes with lead levels exceeding the accepted threshold for safety, and the majority of these children are African-American (Wood, 2003). Many families that are poor live in neighborhoods in core inner cities. Inner city communities more often lack opportunities for parents to build social networks, leading to increased stress and increased child abuse. Furthermore, families are isolated further by the violence and crime that are concentrated in neighborhoods of families with low income.

The lack of safe places for children to congregate and play is a reality faced by many families that are poor throughout the United States. Kids who live in neighborhoods that are poor are less likely to participate in sports or after school activities. In fact, SES ties to children's exposure to environmental risks. Children from economically disadvantaged families often live in neighborhoods with toxic wastes and hazardous pollutants. Research has shown that children from low SES families are more likely to live in a poor environment that has greater exposure to toxic substance and is less conducive for children's development. For example, because SES negatively correlates with tobacco use, children from low SES families are more likely to expose to cigarette smoke at home as compared to their high SES peer (Chen, 2014).

Neighborhoods with high crime are associated with a decrease in youth reporting high levels of physical activity. This is particularly troubling as many minority families particularly Black reside in these neighborhoods. In fact, it is still unclear how long the child must reside in the environment to experience such negative health impacts. Many poor children are vulnerable because of the environment in which they live. Many families that are poor live in neighborhoods with concentrated poverty, such as neighborhoods in the inner city, which are typically neighborhoods of color (Knitzer, 2000). Further research is needed to understand the complex dynamics of health outcomes and duration of exposure to poverty, including neighborhood and environment.

Health Disparities among the Poor

While family poverty status is a key factor underlying racial/ethnic disparities in health, it is not easily explained by other variables. Minority children living in low-income neighborhoods are typically at a higher risk for poor health, primarily due to the negative impact of poverty. Financial hardship, especially among minority children in low-income families, is associated indirectly with a child's health outcomes, suggesting that socioeconomic status does matter both for mothers' psychological functioning and child health outcomes, and this finding corroborates those of other studies who have argued that socioeconomic plays a role in child health outcomes (Jackson et al., 2000).

Even though racial disparities in children's primary care experiences have been documented in the literature, disparities in socioeconomic status, insurance coverage, and language contribute to but do not completely explain, these disparities in health care. Racial disparities in the delivery of health care may be related to patient-provider relationships (Smedley et al., 2003). This should be cause for major concern in both the public policy and public health communities. Improving the health of children requires policies that address the problem of childhood poverty.

Impact of Family/Provider Relationship on Child Health

A child's family is considered important to ensure that the decision-making affecting the health and well-being of children and their families is based on the needs of those children and families. Pediatric visits routinely include the child and the parent, and during that time pediatricians can observe the influence of family on health outcomes and decisions for the child. Experienced pediatricians acquire an intuitive sense of how families shape children's health, and develop recommendations accordingly. Patient-provider relationship factors, such as interpersonal communication, trust, and mutual understanding of cultural differences in health needs and expectations are related to the race and ethnicity of both patient and providers.

Families, because of a number of interacting factors, may be unable to meet the medical or social needs of their children. The family as a unit is so basic and central to the care and welfare of the child that it is highly suggested that pediatricians adopt the concept of family pediatrics. Parents want guidance raising their children, and although they consider pediatricians to be good sources of information and support, they seek their counsel inconsistently. Parents believe that pediatricians are meeting the physical needs of their children, but approximately 80% believe that they could use more information in child rearing (Young et al., 1998; Horwitz et al., 1998). The pediatrician must consider family dynamics when screening for and diagnosing problems and developing a management plan or initiating a referral for a child. It is appropriate for pediatricians to identify the types of support that enhance family stability and function and offer connections to those services and activities.

Role of Pediatricians

Pediatricians can be helpful by thinking more holistically and understanding not only the problems families are dealing with, but also what is necessary for families to be successful. Pediatricians must learn to recognize families'strenghts as well as their needs to help families function optimally. Pediatricians should assess and address the health and well-being of the entire family and not just the child.

Pediatricians can practice family-focused care that includes practices that focus on the family as a unit of intervention, but are not empowering or based on a recognition of family strength and competence. Family-centered care includes the philosophies, principles, and practices that put the family as the driving force of the health care services. Most pediatricians report that they involve families in the decision making around the health care of their child and make an effort to understand the needs of the family as well as the child (American Academy of Pediatrics Taskforce, 2003). Family pediatrics, family-oriented pediatrics, or life family-centered care requires an active partnership between the pediatrician and the family, but it also extends the responsibilities of the pediatrician to include screening, assessment, and referral of parents with physical, emotional, or social problems.

There are endless opportunities for pediatricians that begin to practice family pediatrics to become more involved in the nurturing of the entire family. Pediatricians can provide extensive counseling to referral and resource recommendations and from community to state and national advocacy. Consultation with colleagues, child development experts, school guidance counselors, private foundations, religious organizations, and other organizations that focus on families may help pediatricians become experienced in family pediatrics. Pediatricians have a unique opportunity to assist families and strengthen their ability to meet the needs of their children.

Health Disparities

Among children, significant racial and ethnic disparities in pediatric health visits, access to health care, and utilization of routine medical care exist. It is well understood that a number of factors contribute to these disparities, which include socioeconomic status, low health literacy, and limited health insurance coverage. Black and Hispanic children have lower rates of visits to a pediatrician for ambulatory care visits, less likely to have a usual source of care or a medical home, and have higher rates of poor health outcomes compared to White children (Zur and Jones, 2015). There are national initiatives to reduce health disparities that reaffirm the nation's commitment to the elimination of these issues. For example, the Centers for Disease Control and Prevention, Healthy People 2020 guide has focused attention on the elimination of health disparities in health care utilization. Improving the health of minority children will require a better understanding in the racial disparities in accessing pediatric health services.

Many studies have found that race concordance with a primary care provider is positively associated with participatory decision making, respect, and overall satisfaction. Health care providers of minority children face challenges when promoting health7 behaviors. Primary care providers of children and families that are poor can advocate for them at multiple levels. Advocacy can occur during doctor visits, through outside community involvement, and at higher levels of government. For pediatricians, the most effective way to advocate for the poor is to receive and welcome families that have Medicaid and those without insurance into their practices. Pediatricians can also support poor families by connecting them with services and resources for which they qualify or need in the community.

Pediatricians can also use materials supplied by community programs to screen their families for social and economic risk factors, adding the screening approach to their regular child development and family social screening. Community support services should be viewed by pediatricians as important interventions for families that can have a positive effect on child health and development. Finally, pediatricians can advocate for poor children at the government level by using the American Academy of Pediatrics materials to be a voice for child health issues.

Among children with special health care needs minority parents are more likely than White parents to report that health care services for their children were not easy to access, use, and they were dissatisfied with the care (Ngui and Flores, 2006). Black/White disparities in dissatisfaction with care focuses primarily on the lack of family-centered care. The importance of a partnership between parents and professionals in the support of children with disabilities is widely acknowledged and is one of the key elements of family-centered care. White children report more positive outcomes with health related quality of life, personal well-being, social well-being, and overall health status compared to Black children and there are substantial racial/ethnic disparities in children general health (Wallander et al., 2012). Disparities exist in parent-reported child health status, where Black parent's perception of their child's overall health was poor. It is important to examine and have a better understanding of how a child's family impacts their health behaviors.

DISCUSSION

Whereas one of the overarching goals of Healthy People 2010 is to "eliminate health disparities," both racial and socioeconomic disparities remain profoundly evident among children in the United States. Race, socioeconomic status, and family functioning are strongly related to one another and it is impossible to reduce their impact on health. Understanding these relationships among social conditions and health early in life is critical for optimizing a child's health status and to understand the origins of disparities in health. It is well known that minority children experience poorer health than White children and racial/ethnic health disparities exist, are extensive, pervasive, and persistent.

The health and well-being of children are linked to their parents' physical, emotional and social health. High levels of psychological distress may lead to inadequate or impaired parenting and adverse child health outcomes. While family structure, neighborhood, environment and interaction with the healthcare system has an impact on a child's health outcome and behavior, it is hard to ignore the lasting impact of family income. Children in poor families experience disparities health problems, a higher risk of severe illness and chronic conditions and more limitation of activity than children in more affluent families (Montgomery, Kiely, and Pappas, 1996). The disparity in child health has consequences and implications, not only for the personal achievement and economic self-sufficiency of the individual children but also for the society deprived productive, healthy workers and citizens.

For example, economic hardship had been shown to influence child health outcomes through its effect on parental emotional health/depressive symptoms and parenting behavior (Jackson et al., 2000). Whether the health gap between low-income and higher income children has grown wider as economic and social conditions have worsened is not known. We expect that increased exposure to poverty is associated with worse child health. Further, we expect that the more difficult conditions faced by African American families leads to worse health among African American children compared to white children with equivalent poverty experience.

Children that have increased poverty exposure is associated with poorer child health. That is, children who have spent a greater proportion of their childhood in poverty are more likely to be in worse health. Nonetheless, it is important to keep in mind that greater exposure to poverty is a more common problem for African American children than for white children (Malat, Oh, and Hamilton, 2005).

It is well understood that increased exposure to poverty may affect child health through a complex web of mechanisms. Given the number and magnitude of the health problem faced by poor families including potential multiple disease pathways and sources of morbidity, simply addressing one problem will note reduce morbidity and mortality in the long run. Improving the health of children requires policies that address the problem of childhood poverty. Both poverty and other factors associated with race are related to child health (McGauhey and Starfield, 1993).

REFERENCES

Angley, M, Divney, A, Magriples, U, and T. Kershaw. 2014. "Social support, family functioning and parenting competence in adolescent parents." *Maternal and child health journal*, *19*(1), 67-73.

Bloom, B, Jones, L, and G. Freeman. 2013. "Summary health statistics for U.S. children: National Health Interview Survey, 2012." *National Center for Health Statistics. Vital Health Stat, 10*(258).

Brown, S. 2004. "Family structure and child well-being: The significance of parental cohabitation." *Journal of Marriage and Family, 66*, 351-367.

Bryson, K. and L. Casper. 1999. "Co-residents grandparents and their grandchildren: Grandparent maintained families." U.S. Department of Commerce. Washington, DC.

Chen, J. 2014. "Asthma and child behavioral skills: Does family socioeconomic status matter?" *Social Science & Medicine*, *115*, 38-48.

Edin, K, and L. Lein. 1997. "Making ends meet: How single mothers survive welfare and low-wage work." Russell Sage Foundation. New York, NY.

El-Mohandes, A, Katz, K, El-Khorazaty, N, McNeely, D, Sharps, P, Jarrett, M, Rose, A, White, D, Young, M, Grylack, L, Murray, K, Katta, P, Burroughs, M, Atiyeh, G, Wingrove, B, and A. Herman 2003. "The effect of a parenting education program on the use of preventive pediatric health care services among low-income, minority mothers: A randomized controlled study." *Pediatrics, 111*, 1324-1332.

Entwisle, D. and K. Alexander. 1996. "Family type and children's growth in reading and math over the primary grades." *Journal of Marriage and Family, 58*, 341-355.

Fleming, C, Kim, H, Harachi, T, and R. Catalano. 2002. "Family processes for children in early elementary school as predictors of smoking initiation." *Journal of Adolescent Health, 20*, 184-189.

Foster, E, and A. Kalil. 2007. Living arrangements and children's development in low-income White, Black, and Latino families," *Child Development, 78*(6), 1657-1674.

Hannon, P, Bishop, V, and S. Scrimshaw. 2000. "African-American and Latina Adolescent Mothers' infant feeding decisions and breastfeeding practices: A qualitative study." *Journal of adolescent health, 26*, 399-407.

Horwitz, S, Leaf, P, and J. Leventhal. 1998. "Identification of psychosocial problems in pediatric primary care: do family attitudes make a difference?" *Archives of Pediatric Adolescent Medicine, 152*, 367-371.

Jackson, A, Gunn, J, Huang, C, and M. Glassman. 2000. "Single Mothers in Low-Wage Jobs: Financial Strain, Parenting, and Preschoolers' Outcomes." *Child development*, *71*(5), 1409-1423.

Knitzer, J. 2000. Promoting resilience: Helping young children and parents affected by substance abuse, domestic violence, and depression in the context of welfare reform. Children and welfare reform, Issue Brief 8. National Center for Children in Poverty. New York, NY.

Malat, J, Joo Oh, H, and M. Hamilton. 2005. "Poverty experience, race, and child health." *Public health reports*, *120*(4), 442.

McGauhey, P, and B. Starfield. 1993. "Child health and the social environment of white and black children." *Social Science & Medicine, 36*(7), 867-874.

Minkler, M. and E. Thompson. 2005. "African-American grandparents raising grandchildren: A national study using the Census 2000 American Community Survey." *Journal of Gerontology, 60B*(2), S82-S92.

Montgomery, L, Kiely, J, and G. Pappas. 1996. "The effects of poverty, race, and family structure on US children's health: data from the NHIS, 1978 through 1980 and 1989 through 1991." *American Journal of Public Health. 86*(10), 1401-1405.

Ngui, E, and G. Flores. 2006. "Satisfaction with care and ease of using health care services among parents of children with special health care needs: The role of race/ethnicity, insurance, language, and adequacy of family-centered care." *Pediatrics, 117*, 1184-1196.

Palermo, T, Valrie, C, and C. Karlson. 2014. "Family and parent influences on pediatric chronic pain." American Psychologist, 69(2), 142-152.

Rhoads, S. 2005. "Taking sex differences seriously." Encounter Books. San Francisco, CA.

Rueger, S, Katz, R, Risser, H, and M. Lovejoy. 2007. "Relations between parental affect and parenting behaviors: A meta-analytic review." *Parenting Science and Practice, 11*, 1-33.

Sidora, K, Feldman, J, Serebrisky, D, and A. Spray. 2012. "A multi-factorial model for examining racial and ethnic disparities in acute asthma visits by children." *Annals of Behavioral Medicine, 43*(1), 15-28.

Sipsma, H, Brooks, K, Cole-Lewis, H, and T. Kershaw. 2010. "Like father, like son: The intergenerational cycle of adolescent fatherhood. *American Journal of Public Health, 100*, 517-525.

Skinner, Ma, Haggerty, K, and R. Catalano. 2009. "Parental and peer influences on teen smoking: Are White and Black families different?." *Nicotine & Tobacco Research, 11*(5), 558-563.

Smedley, B, Stith, A, Nelson, A, et al., 2003. "Unequal treatment: Confronting racial and ethnic disparities in health care. National Academy Press. Washington, DC.

Thompson, S, Auslander, W and N. White. 2001. "Comparison of single-mother and two-parent families on metabolic control of children with diabetes." *Diabetes care, 24*(2), 234-238.

Wallander, J, Fradkin, C, Chien, A, Mrug, S, Banspach, S, Davies, S, Elliott, M, Franzini, L, Schuster, M. 2012. "Racial/ethnic disparities in health-related quality of life and health in children are largely mediated by family contextual difference." *Academic pediatrics, 12*(6), 532-538.

Wood, David. 2003. "Effect of child and family poverty on child health in the United States." *Pediatrics, 112*(Supplement 3), 707-711.

Young, K, Davis, K, Schoen, C, and S. Parker. 1998. Listening to parents: A national survey of parents with young children." Archives of Pediatric Adolescent Medicine, 152, 255-262.

Zur, J, and E. Jones. 2015. Racial and ethnic disparities among pediatric patients at Community Health Centers." *Journal of Pediatrics, 167*(4), 847-850.

BIOGRAPHICAL SKETCHES

Crystal N. Piper

Business address:

University of North Carolina Charlotte
Department of Public Health Sciences
9201 University City Boulevard Room 427 F
Charlotte, NC 28223-0001
Phone: (704) 687-5874 Fax: (704) 687-6222
Email: cpiper1@uncc.edu

Education:

Year	University	Degree
2007	University of South Carolina Health Services Research Policy & Management Dissertation: Examination of Racial Disparities in Childhood Asthma Management Practices in the United States	PhD
2003	Des Moines University Medical Center Health Administration	MHA
2002	Des Moines University Medical Center Public Health	MPH
2001	South Carolina State University	BS
Biology		

Professional experience:

Date	Position/Title	Employer
08/2009-Present	Assistant Professor	University of North Carolina at Charlotte Public Health Sciences Charlotte, NC
05/2005-05/2006	Patient Account Manager	Palmetto Health Richland Emergency Department Columbia, Sc
05/2007-05/2009	Post-Doctoral Fellowship Research Associate	University of South Carolina Rural Health Research Center Columbia, SC
01/2005-05/2009	Adjunct Faculty	Benedict College Department of Health Sciences Columbia, SC
08/2004-05/2007	Research Assistant	University of South Carolina SC Health Disparities Institute Columbia, SC
01/2003-01/2004	Health Manager	South Carolina Department of Health Bureau of Air Quality Columbia, SC
11/2001-12/2002	Research Assistant	Iowa Department of Health Office of the Director Des Moines, IA

Peer-reviewed publications:

I am a health services researcher, bringing the rigor of research methods, the value of evidence-based practice, and the experience of community-engaged programs to vulnerable communities to improve their health status locally, nationally, and internationally. My research focuses on three inter-related thematic areas: 1) reducing and eliminating health disparities, 2) improving health equity across the lifespan, and 3) developing community-engaged approaches to address health disparities affecting diverse populations.

Student mentorship: names of students and former student advisees are underlined.

1. Piper, C., Chalakalal. S., Warren-Findlow, J., Thompson, M., Sebestian, N. (2014) Race, socioeconomic status, HRQoL, and self-management of Type 2 diabetes mellitus among adults in North Carolina. *Southern Medical Journal.* April 2015. 108(4):212-216.
2. Piper, C., Polite-Middleton, T., Chalakalal, S., Sebestian, N., Martin, F. (2015) Race, socioeconomic status, and rurality influences on type 2 diabetes management among North Carolina adults. *Ethnicity & Disease.* Winter 2015.25:46-51.
3. Elder, K., Rice, S., Dean, C., Piper, C. Addressing the differences by race in analgesia use among pediatric patients attending emergency departments. *Journal of Pediatrics.* 3(165). 434-436.
4. Moore, T., Dotson, E., Dean, C., Rice, S., Piper, C. Johns, M., Elder, K. (2014) An assessment of minority faculty in healthcare administration programs. *Journal of Health Administration Education.* Summer 2014:283-296.
5. Elder, K., Gilbert, K., Hanke, L., Dean, C., Rice, S., Johns, M., Piper, C., Wiltshire, J., Moore, T., Wang, J. (2014) Disparities in confidence to manage chronic diseases in men. *AIMS Journal.* 1(3):123-136.
6. Saffari,M., Amini, N., Eftekhar, A., Sanaeinasab, H., Mahmoudi, M., Piper, C. (2013) Educational intervention on health related lifestyle changes among Iranian adolescents. *Iranian Journal of Public Health.* 42(2):172-81.
7. Piper, C., Polite-Middleton, T., Warren-Findlow, J., Thompson, M., Sebastian, N., Akindahunsi, Y. (2013) Racial influences on diabetes management among adults in North Carolina. *Ethnicity and Disease.* 23(3):316-321.
8. Saffari, M., Pakpour, A., Naderi, M., Koenig, H., Baldacchino, D., Piper, C. (2013) Spiritual coping, religiosity, and quality of life: A study of Muslim patients undergoing hemodialysis. *Nephrology.* 18(4):269-275.
9. Alexander, D., Huber, L., Piper, C., Tanner, A. (2013) The association between recreational parks, facilities and childhood obesity: a cross-

sectional study of the 2007 National Survey of Children's Health. *Journal of Epidemiology and Community Health*. 67(5):427-431.
10. Saffari, M., Pakpour, A., Amini, N., Eftekhar, H., Sanaeinasab, H., Mahmoudi, M., Piper, C. (2012) A model based educational intervention to increase physical activity among Iranian adolescents. *Jornal de Pediatria*. 88(5):430-8.
11. Piper, C., Glover, S., Williams, E., Olatosi, B., Charlemagne, S., Campbell, D.,Ogbuano, C., Annang, L., Lee, W., Onsomu, E. (2012) Beliefs and perception of risks among women that have never been tested for HIV in the United States. *Journal of the National Medical Association.* 104:9-10.
12. Onsomu, E., Piper, C., Moore, D., Timmons, S. (2012) Association between education and domestic violence among women being offered an HIV test in urban and rural areas in Kenya. *Journal of Interpersonal Violence*. 27(10):2022-2038.
13. Goodwin, John. Sage Secondary Data Analysis - Sage Library of Research Methods Series. Piper, C., Glover, S., Elder, K., Baek, J., Wilkinson, L. (2011) Disparities in access to care among asthmatic children in relation to race and socioeconomic status. *Sage Publications*. 271-279.
14. Elder, K., McRoy, L., Horn, W., Ahmed, S., Hullett, S., Allison, J., Piper, C. (2011) Trust, medication adherence, and hypertension control in Southern African American men. *American Journal Public Health.* 102(12): 2242-2245.
15. Glover, S., Piper, C., Hassan, R., Preston, G., Wilkinson, L., Bowen-Seabrook, J., Mayer-Davis, B., Williams, S. (2011) Dietary, physical activity, and lifestyle behaviors of rural African American South Carolina children. *Journal of the National Medical Association.* 103(4):300-4.
16. Glover, S., Piper, C., Williams, E., Bennett, K., Thompson, W., Annang, L., Charlemagne, S., Hassan, R. (2010) Preventable asthma episodes among urban/rural children and adolescents: A comparative study. *Journal of Health Disparities Research and Practice*. 4(2):41-49.
17. Piper, C., Glover, S., Elder, K., Baek, J., Wilkinson, L. (2010) Disparities in access to care among asthmatic children in relation to race and socioeconomic status. *Journal of Child Health Care.* 14(3):271-279.
18. Glover, S., Rivers, P., Asoh, D., Piper, C., Murph, K. (2010) Data mining for health executive decision support: An imperative with a daunting future! *Royal Society of Medicine*. 23:42-6.

19. Piper, C., Glover, S., Elder, K., Baek, J., Fernandez, S. (2010) Disparities between asthma management and insurance type among children. *Journal of the National Medical Association.* 102(7):556-561.
20. Glover, S., Xirasagar, S., Jeon, Y., Elder, K., Piper, C., Pastides, H. (2009) A human capital approach to reduce health disparities. *Journal of Health Disparities Research and Practice.* 3(1):1-14.
21. Piper, C., Elder, K., Glover, S., Baek, J. (2008) Examination of racial disparities in childhood asthma management practices in the United States. *Journal of Health Disparities Research and Practice.* 2(3): 1-16.
22. Piper, C., Elder, K., Glover, S., Baek, J. (2008) Racial influences associated with asthma management of episodes among children in the United States. *Ethnicity and Disease.* 18(2):225-227.
23. Glover, S., Elder, K., Xirasagar, S. Baek, J., Piper, C., Campbell, D. (2007) Mental health utilization among persons with chronic diseases. *Journal of Health Disparities Research and Practice.* 1(3):45-65.
24. Elder, K., Xirasagar, S., Bowen, S., Miller, N., Glover, S., Piper, C. (2007) Why African Americans did not evacuate before hurricane Katrina? A Qualitative Study of Evacuees from New Orleans. *American Journal of Public Health.* 97(1):124-129.
25. Campbell, D., Piper, C., Elder, K., Williams, D., Lloyd, S. (2006) Faith based approach to reduce colorectal cancer disparities: Community based participatory research in action. *Cancer Epidemiology Biomarkers & Prevention.* 15(12 supplement). B40.

Manuscripts in preparation:

1. Piper, C., Sebastion, N. Understanding overall health status and child oral health outcomes in the United States.
2. Piper, C., Shah, S., Bankapur, J., Racine, E., Platonova, E. Perceptions of health among adults with arthritis in North Carolina.
3. Piper, C., Tanner, A., Yadok, Z., Sebastian, N., Allen, C., Shah, S. HIV testing behaviors among pregnant women in North Carolina: a cross-sectional study using 2008 PRAMS.
4. Piper, C., Allen, C., Cherry, N., Coffman, M., Platonova, E. Age differences in sexual partnerships and its association with sexually transmitted infections in minority young adults.
5. Piper, C., Allen, C. Black Family Influences on Child Health (Book Chapter).

6. Piper, C., Glover, S., Williams, E., Olatosi, B., Charlemagne, S., Campbell, D.,Ogbuano, C., Annang, L., Lee, W., Onsomu, E. Piper, C. Characteristics, health behaviors, and the utilization of HIV testing services among women in the United States.
7. Piper, C., Tsovinar, L., Swayampakala, K. Complementary and Alternative medicine use among adults with chronic diseases in the US.
8. Piper, C., Tsovinar, L., Allen, C. Attitudes and Beliefs about Gynecological Health & Cervical Cancer Screening: the college women health study.
9. Piper, C., Donigan, W., Hammersmith, K. Gaston County Healthy Smiles Child Dental Health Home Project.
10. Piper, C., Able, W., McCord, L., Cornelius, J., Yang, A., Davis, C., Drew-Branch, V. Conference Proceedings: Assessing Health Disparities in Mecklenburg County, NC.

Refereed presentations at national conferences:

1. Harver, A. Davis, Piper, C. Portwood, S. Zuber, P. Platonova, E. "The BSPH Capstone e-Portfolio: documenting effective communication and critical thinking skills." Association of Programs in Public Health. Washington, DC. March 2015. Poster Presentation.
2. Piper, C., Elder, K., Onsomu, E., Sebastian, N., Chalakalal, S., Shah, S., Glover, S. "Characteristics, health behaviors, and the utilization of HIV testing services among women in the United States." 1st Annual North Carolina State Representative Beverly Earle Health Disparities Conference. February 2015.
3. Tanner, A., Ma, A., Jenkins, W., Allen, C., Young, A., Piper, C. "Individuals and structural factors affecting care linkage and engagement for HIV-positive individuals." 141st Annual Public Health Association Meeting & Exposition. Boston, MA. October 2013. Oral Presentation.
4. Yadok, Z., Tanner, A., Piper, C., Thompson, M. "HIV testing behaviors among

   pregnant women in North Carolina: a cross-sectional study using 2008 PRAMS." 140th Annual Public Health Association Meeting & Exposition. San Francisco, CA. October 2012. Poster Presentation.
5. Piper, C., Chalakalal, S., Thompson, M., Warren-Findlow, J. "Management of type II diabetes mellitus and health related quality of life among adults in North Carolina." 139th Annual Public Health Association

Meeting & Exposition. Washington, DC. October 2011. Poster Presentation.

6. Taylor, Y., Laditika, J., Piper, C. "Emergency department use for childhood asthma: comparing rural and urban areas." Academy Health Annual Research Meeting. Orlando, FL. June 2012. Poster Presentation.
7. Onsomu, E., Piper, C., Moore, D., Timmons, S. "Underestimating HIV acquisition perceived risk in Kenya: sexual-risk taking in urban and rural areas." 138th Annual Public Health Association Meeting & Exposition., CO. November 2010. Poster Presentation.
8. Piper, C., Glover, S., Swayampakala, K., Ogbuanu, C., Wilkinson, L., Campbell, D. "Role of spirituality in the use of CAM therapies among adults with chronic diseases in the United States." 137th Annual Public Health Association Meeting & Exposition. Philadelphia, PA. November 7-11, 2009. Poster Presentation.
9. Piper, C., Glover, S., Harutyunyan, T., Williams, E. Predictors underlying disparities of cervical cancer screening among somen in the United States." 137th Annual Public Health Association Meeting & Exposition. Philadelphia, PA. November 7-11, 2009. Poster Presentation.
10. Williams, E., Bellinger, J., Campbell, D., Olatosi, B., Piper, C., Wright, B. "A pipeline project to enhance HBCU student led research projects." 136th Annual Public Health Association Meeting & Exposition. San Diego, CA. October 25-29, 2008. Oral Presentation.
11. Campbell, D., Olatosi, B., Bellinger, J., Piper, C. Williams, E., Glover, S., Wright. B. "Development of a pipeline project to increase student led research projects in health." 136th Annual Public Health Association Meeting & Exposition. San Diego, CA. October 25-29, 2008. Paper Presentation.
12. Piper, C., Glover, S., Olatosi, B., Charlemagne, S., Campbell, D., Ogbuano, C., Williams, E., Annang, L., Wilson, S., Lee, W. "Beliefs and perception of risks among women that have never been tested for HIV in the United States" Academy for Health Equity Conference. Denver, CO. June 26-28, 2008. Poster Presentation.
13. Williams, D., Elder, K., Lloyd, S. Piper, C. "Faith based approach to address colon cancer among African Americans in South Carolina." 11TH Biennial Symposium on Minorities, the Medically Underserved & Cancer. Washington, DC. April 3-6, 2008. Poster Presentation.
14. Piper, C., Glover, S., Elder, K., Baek, J., Fernandez, S. "Association of asthma management and insurance type among children in the United States." 3rd Annual Columbia University Teachers College Health

Disparities Conference. New York, NY. March 7-8, 2008. Paper Presentation.

15. Piper, C., Elder, K., Glover, S., Baek, J. "Racial influences associated with asthma management of episodes among children in the United States." 13th Annual Centers for Disease Control and Prevention Maternal Child Health Epidemiology Conference. Atlanta, GA. December 10-11, 2007. Poster Presentation.
16. Piper, C., Glover, S., Elder, K., Baek, J. "Examination of racial disparities in childhood asthma management practices in the United States." 135th Annual Public Health Association Meeting & Exposition. Washington, DC. November 3-7, 2007. Paper Presentation.
17. Campbell, D., Elder, K., Glover, S., Piper, C. "Examination of racial disparities in comorbidities among five-year breast cancer survivors in South Carolina." Minority Women's Health Summit. Washington, DC. August 23-26, 2007. Poster Presentation.
18. Elder, K., Xirasagar, S., Bowen, S.A., Maitra, D., Piper, C., Campbell, D. "Disparities in
    Hurricane Katrina evacuation: factors in African Americans' evacuation response." Academy Health Annual Research Meeting. Seattle, WA. June 25-27, 2006. Poster Presentation.
19. Glover, S., Piper, C. "USC-Claflin Center of Excellence for the Elimination of
    Health Disparities in HIV and Cancer: saving our community one step at a time." evaluation of community connections: Using Research Results to Reduce Health Disparities National EXPORT Health Conference. Wintergreen, VA. June 25-28 2007. Paper Presentation.
20. Piper, C., Glover, S., Elder, K., Baek, J. "Exploration of race-based disparities in access to care among children with asthma in the United States." 133rd Annual Public Health Association Meeting & Exposition. Philadelphia, PA. December 10-14, 2005. Poster Presentation.

Invited presentations:

1. **Piper, C.** "Social Determinants of Health." University of South Carolina. November 13, 2014.
2. **Piper, C**. Lilburn, L. Wilson, B. "Role of prevention and access to health care in reducing health disparities." Charlotte Talks WFAE 90.7 National Public Radio Charlotte, NC. April 2, 2012. Live Radio Commentary.

3. **Piper, C.**, Glover, S., Olatosi, B., Charlemagne, S., Campbell, D., Ogbuano, C., Williams, E., Annang, L., Wilson, S., Lee, W. "Beliefs and perception of risks among women that have never been tested for HIV in the United States" Academy for Health Equity Conference. Denver, CO. June 26-28, 2008. Poster Presentation (Invited).
4. **Piper, C.**, Campbell, D. "What is Public Health?" Gospel WFMV 95.3 Radio Broadcast. Columbia, SC. April 21, 2008. Live Radio Commentary.
5. Glover, S., **Piper, C.** "Perspectives on EXPORT Centers." Evaluation of Community Connections: using research results to reduce health disparities in National EXPORT Health Conference. Wintergreen, VA. June 25-28 2007. Plenary Panel Presentation.
6. **Piper, C.**, Glover, S., Elder, K., Baek, J. "Exploration of race-based disparities in access to care among children with asthma in the United States." 11th Annual Centers for Disease Control and Prevention Maternal Child Health Epidemiology Conference. Miami, FL. December 7-9, 2005. Plenary Panel Presentation.

Funding

Internal:

Role: Principal Investigator Amount: $6,000
Funding Agency: University of North Carolina Charlotte Faculty Research Grant
Year: 2014-2017
Title: Gaston County Healthy Smiles Child Dental Home Project

Role: Principal Investigator Amount: $1,000
Funding Agency: University of North Carolina Charlotte Chancellor's Diversity Grant
Year: 2014-2015
Title: NC Representative Beverly Earle Health Disparities Distinguished Lecture

Role: Principal Investigator Amount: $1,000
Funding Agency: University of North Carolina Charlotte Chancellor's Diversity Grant
Year: 2010-2011

Title: Project PACE: **P**ublic Health **A**cademic & **C**areer **E**nrichment Program

Role: Principal Investigator Amount: $6,000
Funding Agency: University of North Carolina Charlotte Faculty Research Grant
Year: 2010-2012
Title: Attitudes and Beliefs about Gynecological Health & Cervical Cancer Screening: The College Women's Health Study

External:

Role: Principal Investigator Amount: $3,000
Funding Agency: Mecklenburg County Health Department
Year: 2014-2015
Title: Mecklenburg County Health Department & Carolina's Healthcare System Partnership Impact Study

Teaching:

University of North Carolina at Charlotte
Undergraduate
HLTH 3105 Public Health Education and Promotion (BSPH Required Course)
HLTH 3101 Foundations of Public Health (Pre-Public Health Required Course)
HLTH 3000 Independent Study (BSPH Elective Course)
HLTH 4000 Race/Ethnicity, Poverty, & Health Disparities (Elective Course)

Graduate
HLTH 6204 Research Methods (MSPH Required Course)
HLTH 6221 Community Health (MSPH Required Course)
HADM 6128 Human Resource Management (MHA Required Course)
HLTH 6000 Race/Ethnicity, Poverty, & Health Disparities (Elective Course)

Dissertation Committee Member
Steven Hardy, Health-related disparities in pediatric asthma: morbidity, attitudes toward illness, and symptom perception, PhD Health Psychology Completed 2012.

Julie Covington, Efficacy of webinar training for school personnel continuing professional education, EdD Educational Leadership Completed 2012.

Michele Rodriguez-Diaz, Bicultural context and metabolic health in bariatric patients, PhD Health Psychology. In Progress.

Tamara Scott, A combined intervention to treat binge eating and overweight or obesity in African American women with binge eating disorder, PhD Health Psychology. In Progress.

Eric Junious, HIV and state prisons, PhD Health Services Research. In Progress.

Sharon MacKinnon, The association of race and religiosity with the contraceptive behavior of women having abortions in 2008. PhD Health Services Research. In Progress.

Thesis Chair

Tatreka Polite, Race, socioeconomic status, & rural/urban geographic disparities in the management of diabetes among adults in North Carolina, MSPH Completed 2011.

Shilpa Chakalaka, Management of type II diabetes mellitus & health related quality of life among sdults in North Carolina, MSPH Completed 2011.

Jyoti Bankapur, Perceptions of health among adults with arthritis in North Carolina, MSPH Completed 2011.

Purva Korgaonkar, Program evaluation plan for the Mobile 1000 program of the Wockhardt Foundation, MSPH Completed 2013.

Bradley Williams, Lupus education and awareness program (LEAP), MSPH Completed 2013.

Natay Cherry, Age differences in sexual partnerships and its association with sexually transmitted infections in minority young adults, MSPH Completed 2014.

Tiffany Martin, Making DOPE (Determined, Optimistic, Purposeful, Engaged Decisions!) To Reduce STIs in Adolescents in Mecklenburg County, MSPH Completed 2014.

Gregory Scarola, Physical activity among older diabetes in North Carolina, MSPH. In Progress

Thesis Committee Member

Dayna Alexander, The association between recreational parks facilities and childhood obesity: A cross-sectional study Of 2007 National Survey Of Children's Health (NSCH) Participants, MSPH Completed 2010.

Tamara Hawkins, Community service grant proposal: reducing HIV transmission among high risk minority youth & adolescents, MSPH Completed 2010.

Leah Broadhurst, The association of STD counseling and/or testing and consistent condom use: a cross-sectional study of 2006-2008 National Survey of Family Growth, MSPH Competed 2011.

Zenret Yadok, HIV testing behaviors among pregnant women in North Carolina: a cross-sectional study using 2008 PRAMS, MSPH Completed 2011.

Jacob Mangum, Effect of race/ethnicity on diabetes diagnosis based on HbA1c and HOMA levels, MSPH Completed 2012.

Brandon Christensen, Cognitive ability and functionality in older adults, MSPH. In Progress.

Jacqueline Mungo, Freedom Schools of Charlotte, NC, MSPH. In Progress.

University of South Carolina:

Graduate

HADM 528 Organizational Behavior in Health Care (MHA Required Course)

enedict College:

Undergraduate

HE 230 Stress Management (Elective Course)

HE 230 Health Education (Elective Course)

Advanced professional development:

2009 NVIVO Software

2010 Robert Wood Johnson Foundation Coaching Clinic

2011 Robert Wood Johnson Foundation Coaching Clinic

2012 National Center for Health Statistics (NCHS) Secondary Datasets

2013 UNC Charlotte Project Mosaic STATA Workshop

2014 UNC Charlotte Project Mosaic R Workshop

2015 University of Michigan Structural Equation Modeling

Honors and awards:

1997 Scholarship, American Business Women's Association

1997 Academic Award, South Carolina State University

2001 Member, Who's Who among American Students
2001 Columbia Urban League Young, Talented, Gifted Award
2004 W. K. Kellogg Fellow University of South Carolina
2004 Chancellor's List of America for Academic Excellence
2013 UNC Charlotte College of Health & Human Services Teaching Excellence Nominee
2014 UNC Charlotte Disability Services Outstanding Faculty Award
2015 UNC Charlotte College of Health & Human Services Community Engagement Award

Professional leadership & service:

National

American Public Health Association (APHA)

Member, Community Health Planning & Policy Development (2004-Present)

Governing Councilor (Elected), Executive Board (2009-2011)

Policy Co-Chair, Community Health Planning & Policy Development (2006-2008)

Grant Proposal Reviewer

Health Resources and Services Administration (HRSA) (2006-Present)

Journal Reviewer

Journal of the National Medical Association – (2006-Present)
Ethnicity & Disease (2006-Present)
Journal of Healthcare for the Poor and Underserved – (2008-Present)
North Carolina Medical Journal – (2010-Present)
Journal of Rural Health – (2010-Present)
American Journal of Reproductive Health – (2012-Present)

Professional Memberships

American College of Health Care Executives, Chicago, Illinois, (2001-2004)
Academy Health, Washington, DC, (2005-Present)
South Carolina Public Health Association (2006-Present)
Member, International Child Health Network, New Delhi, India, (2010-Present)
Member, South Carolina Food Task Force, Columbia, SC (2013-Present)

University of North Carolina Charlotte

Strong Women of UNCC, Advisor (Elected), (2011-Present)

Safe Zone Ally, Advisor, (2010-Present)

Organization Web Communications, Committee Member (Appointed), (2010-2011)

Bookstore Advisory Group, Member, (2009-2010)

College of Health and Human Services

Scholarship Committee Member, (2010-Present)

Common Course Committee Member, (2010-2011)

Faculty Legacy Committee Member, (2012-Present)

Q City Metro Contributor Member, (2012-Present)

Administrative Faculty Fellow Program, (2015-Present)

Public Health Sciences Department

MHA Program Committee Member, (2009-Present)

Graduate Faculty Member, (2009-Present)

Health Services Research Faculty Member, (2009-Present

Health Psychology Affiliate Faculty Member, (2009-Present)

Upsilon Phi Delta, Advisor, (2011-Present)

BSPH Program Committee Member, (2012-2013)

Volunteer services/extracurricular activities:

Student Mentor – Richland County School District One – (2001-Present) – Columbia, SC

Peer Educator – Midlands Area Health Club – (1996-2001) – Columbia, SC

Active Band Member – South Carolina State University – (1997-2001) – Orangeburg, SC

Evaluator – Columbia Urban League – (2005-Present) – Columbia, SC

Volunteer – Salvation Army – (2006-2007) – Columbia, SC

Volunteer – Big Brother/Big Sister – (2007-Present), Columbia, SC

Committee Co-Chair – Healthy Columbia Campaign – (2010-2012), Columbia, SC

Researcher/Evaluator – C. W. Williams Health Center – (2013-Present), Charlotte, NC

Volunteer – Mecklenburg County United Way Young Leaders – (2013-Present) Charlotte, NC

Corliss Allen Solomon

Name: Corliss Allen Solomon, MPH

Affiliation: Doctoral Student at UNC Charlotte

Address: Department of Public Health Sciences, UNC Charlotte
9201 University City Blvd, Charlotte, NC, 28223

Education: University of North Carolina at Charlotte
Charlotte, NC
PhD in Public Health Science, May 2018

Florida A &M University, *Institute of Public Health* Tallahassee, FL
Master of Public Health, May 2009

Florida A &M University, *College of Arts & Sciences* Tallahassee, FL
Bachelor of Science in Psychology, August 2007

Research and Professional Experience:

University of North Carolina at Charlotte August 2014 – Present
Research Graduate Assistant, Charlotte, NC

- Serve as an assistant evaluator for the CDC Racial and Ethnic Approaches to Community Health
- Project manager for the Kids in Parks-UNCC data collection
- Assist and contribute to the development of manuscripts for the peer review process
- Foster key linkages between the minority community and academia
- Assist in analyzing data in statistical software

Micromass Communication December 2012 - August 2014
Behaviorist within Strategic Services, Cary, NC

- Develop, plan and assess multi-channel health education programs

- Design the behavioral science foundation and curriculum for patient and healthcare professional campaigns
- Uncover key behavioral insights to inform campaign strategy
- Manage internal and external behavioral research initiatives, including research design, survey/guide development, analysis, and vendor relationship
- Consult with both internal company and external client teams, providing customer behavioral insights and strategy recommendations throughout program lifecycles
- Develop program measurement plans that provide the framework for capturing key outcomes

Centers for Disease Control & Prevention October 2009 — October 2012
Public Health Prevention Service Fellow, Atlanta, GA

PHPS is a 3 year training and service fellowship for master's level public health professionals. The fellowship focuses on public health program management and provides experience in program planning, implementation, and evaluation through specialized hands-on training and mentorship at CDC, and in national, state and local health organizations. Training and experience is gained through two-6 month rotations at CDC, and a two year field placement at a public health agency/organization.

Mecklenburg County Health Department October 2010 — October 2012
CDC PHPS 2-Year Field Placement- Health Promotion Branch
Charlotte, NC

- Researched and prepared communication, materials and marketing programs, projects, activities and strategies for the Mecklenburg County Fruit & Vegetable Coalition using relevant communication theories and models.
- Plan, organize, direct and evaluate prevention project and activities for the Health Promotion Branch including programming targeting chronic diseases, physical activity, nutrition, and mental health
- Exercised full administrative and management responsibility and authority for conducting communication interventions while leading development, testing, grants, audience research and dissemination of a

breastfeeding education video for local WIC clinics using state-of-the-art technology
- Facilitated focus group, use audience segmentation analysis and formative research to select appropriate communication channels to increase care engagement among HIV patients
- Develop, tests, and disseminates health related and educational materials and information for public awareness and for specific lay audiences such as newsletters, web content, articles, brochures, videos and social media messaging for diverse audiences including the public, stakeholders, political and community leaders
- Arrange communication of health related media on social media platforms
- Provide training programs for professional staff and colleagues quarterly on Health promotion topics
- Establish and maintain effective working relationships with stakeholders while serving as the communication liaison for a number of coalitions and programming related to nutrition, physical activity, heart disease, diabetes, and access to healthcare
- Review and edit materials developed by staff to ensure accuracy and program objectives are being met
- Identified, analyzed and created health department website reports and briefings for the management team
- Provide subject matter expertise and technical assistance to the management of social media efforts for the local jurisdictional levels.
- Use audiovisual production expertise as liaison between program staff and video and creative production staff

Office of Public Health Preparedness and Response
April 2010 — October 2010
CDC PHPS 6-Month Rotation- Division of Strategic National Stockpile
Atlanta, GA

- Coordinated health media production (e.g., graphics, broadcast production) for risk communication activities and training videos
- Led theoretically-based, practical communication training sessions for state and local emergency preparedness planners and public information officers
- Developed presentation materials for meetings and trainings

- Created an Evaluation Guide for SNS Recruitment Kits
- Maintained effective working relationships within and outside the division to accomplish division goals
- Communicated information through presentations to internal and external stakeholders and customers

Agency for Toxic Substances and Disease Registry
October 2009 — April 2010
CDC PHPS 6-Month Rotation- Division of Health Assessment
Atlanta, GA

- Conducted needs assessments to identify communication priorities and needs among participants in the Petition Program
- Analyzed data, identified gaps and provided recommendations to fill health communication-based gaps
- Developed, implemented and maintained health communication procedures for the Petition Program
- Created and implemented a monthly newsletter for lay audiences for a health communication initiative within the Petition Program
- Conducted audience research, collected feedback from participants and created a strategic plan to address participants requests within the Petition Program
- Presented results of research and evaluation activities to stakeholders

US Department of Health and Human Services January 2009 – May 2009
Office on Women's Health Region IV Intern
Atlanta, GA

- Revitalized collegiate contributions towards the 2009 Women's Health Strategic Work Plan
- Headed strategic planning for addressing the health disparity among infant mortality in Region 4
- Researched and documented policy changes affecting minority women in Region 4

Professional Appointments:

2007 Intern, NIH Minority Summer Research Experience
2009 Region IV Intern, Office on Women's Health
2009 - 2012 Fellow, CDC, Public Health Prevention Service (PHPS)
2012 - 2014 Behaviorist, MicroMass Communications
2014 - Research Assistant, University of North Carolina at Charlotte

Honors:

2007 Florida Big Bend AHEC Community Health Scholar
2008 Florida Health Alliance on Diversity Scholar
2009 Dr. Satcher Public Health leadership Award, Florida A & M University
2009 - 2012 CDC's Public Health Prevention Service Fellow
2014 - 2015 Wayland H. Cato Jr. First-Year Doctoral Fellowship, University of North Carolina at Charlotte

Publications (last 3 years):

Montana J, Stoutenberg M, Racine E, **Allen C**, West JL. (2016) Adapting the Exercise is Medicine Model for Community-Based Primary Health Care Clinics. *Med Sci Sports Exerc*;48:5 Supplement

Allen, C., Lopez, I., Dutton, M. & Crowther, V. (2015) The Cognitive Mediating Process of Diabetes among African-American College Students *Florida Public Health Review*; 12, 69-77.

In: Socioeconomic Status
Editor: Geoffrey Perkins

ISBN: 978-1-63485-326-2

Chapter 4

ATTITUDES TOWARD SOCIOECONOMIC STATUS: INEQUALITY, POVERTY AND THE WELFARE STATE IN THE UNITED STATES

Carol Schmid*
Professor of Sociology, Guilford Technical Community College, Jamestown, North Carolina, US

ABSTRACT

Inequality and poverty are issues that deeply divide the American public when it comes to the role that the government should play in alleviating these dual problems. Despite lower unemployment and an improving economy many Americans are more pessimistic currently than after the 2008 financial crisis that the American Dream is out of reach. The first section of the paper analyzes attitudes toward poverty and the government safety net programs in relationship to income and party affiliation. In general the public is severely split in views on poverty and safety net policies. Most scholars agree that wealth inequality in the United States is at historic highs. Disagreements about wealth inequality enter into policy debates ranging from welfare to taxation. How do Americans see the optimal level of wealth inequality? Most individuals see inequality growing between rich and poor but differ in solutions. In general emerging and developing countries are more optimistic than rich countries about the future. The second section investigates theories to

* clschmid@gtcc.edu.

better understand the polarized attitudes toward socioeconomic status, inequality and poverty in America. The final section evaluates the implication of public attitudes for social policy.

Inequality and poverty are issues that deeply divide the American public when it comes to the role that the government should play in alleviating these dual problems. Despite lower unemployment and an improving economy many Americans are more pessimistic in 2015 than after the 2008 financial crisis. Americans are concerned that the American Dream is out of reach. Most scholars agree that wealth inequality in the United States is at historic highs (Saez 2013, Saez and Zucman 2014, Fry and Kochhar 2014, Grusky and MacLean 2016). Between 2009 and 2012 gains were very uneven - individuals in the top 1 percent saw their income grow by 31.4 percent while the bottom 99 percent of individuals captured only .4 percent (Saez 2013).

Poverty and inequality are undergirded by attitudes. Public support is needed to sustain institutions that increase or sustain inequality. The first section of the paper analyzes attitudes toward inequality and poverty in relationship to income, social class, race, gender and party affiliation. Attitudes toward the American Dream and it possibility are also evaluated over time. The second section investigates polls and theories to better understand the polarized attitudes toward socioeconomic status, inequality and poverty in America. The final section evaluates the implication of public attitudes for social policy.

American Attitudes Toward Inequality, Poverty, and the American Dream

There are several ways in which poverty and inequality are supported by attitudes. Public support is necessary to sustain policies which allow the gap between rich and middle and poor classes to be sustained. For example, a low minimum wage or the tax code that give advantages to upper incomes must be seen as legitimate.

Disagreements about wealth inequality enter into policy debates ranging from welfare to taxation. A substantial majority of Americans believe that the gap between rich and poor has widened. A 2012 Pew Research Center survey (Americans see growing gap between rich and poor 2013) found that 65 percent of Americans believed inequality increased over the last decade. Most

(57 percent) Americans believed this was a bad thing. There are significant divisions between different sectors of the American public in why people are poor (see Table 1).

Table 1.

More often to blame if a person is poor	Circumstances	Lack of Effort
Race		
Black	62%	28%
Hispanic	59%	27%
White	41%	41%
Gender among whites		
Men	34%	50%
Women	48%	34%
Family Income		
$75,000 +	41%	40%
$30,000-$75,000	40%	43%
Less than $30,000	58%	31%
Education		
College graduate +	47%	33%
Some college	33%	49%
HS or less	43%	42%
Political Orientation		
Republican	28%	57%
Democrat	61%	24%

Source: Pew Research Center (2013).

Figures do not add up to 100%. Both circumstances, lack of effort and don't know are not provided.

The largest gaps are related to race, income, party affiliation with a somewhat smaller gap between white men and women. The Pew question asked a representative sample of Americans why people are poor, is it related to circumstances, lack of effort or both? Among black respondents there was a 34 percent gap with most (62 percent) saying 'circumstances' rather than 'lack of effort' (28 percent). Whites were almost evenly split between these two answers. Hispanics were closer to blacks with 32 percent favoring 'circumstances' (59 percent) over 'lack of effort' (27 percent) (Americans see growing gap between rich and poor 2013).

Feagins (1975) in an earlier analysis of opinion polls found white Protestants and Catholics, people with middle-income earnings, and those with moderate levels of education favored individualistic over structural explanations of poverty whereas the reverse pattern emerged for African Americans, low income earners and those with less education. He did not foresee the striking partisan divisions.

In the Pew 2012 poll there was a significant gap between those identifying as Republican or Democrats. While Republicans strongly favored 'lack of effort' (57 percent) over 'circumstances' (28 percent), the opposite profile characterized Democrats. Among self-identified Democrats 61 percent said that 'circumstances' were much more important than 'lack of effort' (24 percent). Among white men and women the gap was somewhat smaller. However the sexes came out on opposite sides of why people are poor. A majority of white men (50 percent) named 'lack of effort' as opposed to white women who believed that 'circumstances' (48 Percent) played a larger role. The wide gaps in opinions about why people are poor make it very difficult to formulate consistent welfare programs. There seems little common ground between Democrats and Republicans and those more and less privileged according to social class. Well off families with an income of $75,000 or more and poor who have a family income of less than $30,000 also viewed poverty in significantly different ways. While higher income families believed that 'circumstances' and 'lack of effort' played an equal roll those earning less than $30,000 selected circumstances over lack of effort by a 27 percent margin (Americans see growing gap between rich and poor 2013).

The American public sees rising conflict between rich and poor. The Pew Social and Demographic Trends (2012) asked how much conflict there is between rich and poor, from very strong conflicts to no conflicts on a four point scale in December 2011. The same question was asked in 2009. The perceptions of conflict over time has increased and become more intense. Thirty percent of Americans in 2011 said that there are 'very strong' conflicts between rich and poor. That is double the proportion who gave a similar response in 2009. The perceptions of class conflicts have increased in all income groups.

Age and political orientation are important variables in viewing the conflict between rich and poor. In 2011 younger individuals from 18-34 were over 15 percent more likely to perceive a very strong or strong conflict between rich and poor than seniors 65 years and over (71 percent versus 55 percent). The question on class conflict is also polarized by political orientation. While only 55 percent of Republicans say there is a 'very strong' or 'strong conflict' between rich and poor Democrats overwhelmingly (73 percent) agree with this statement. This is related to the view of the Republican Party. In a 2012 survey more than 60 percent of Americans said the GOP favors the rich over the middle class and poor (Pew Research Center, Social and Demographic Trends, 2012).

The Pew representative survey in July 2012 (Pew Research Center, Social and Demographic Trends, 2012) confirms the vastly different opinions on taxes. The partisan gap between Republican and Democrats is significant. Republicans believe that upper-income people pay their fair share in taxes (44 percent) while only 13 percent of Democrats concur in this belief. An overwhelming 78 percent of Democrats say that upper-income people pay too little in federal taxes. The lack of consensus between the parties makes it both difficult to govern and to compromise on welfare policies and taxes. Curtis and Anderson (2015) observe that compared to individuals in high economic positions, those in lower economic positions are much less likely to perceive inequality as fair.

In 1926 F. Scott Fitzgerald wrote "Let me tell you about the very rich. They are different from you and me…." (335, 1989). The rich or upper class still appears to have an easier and more enjoyable life, at least according to results from the 2012 Pew Research Center, Social and Demographic Trends study. Upper class Americans reported being more happy with their life overall (42 percent) in relationship to the middle class (32 percent) and lower class (20 percent). Class also makes a difference with respect to stress. The upper class described their life as rarely/never experiencing stress (33 percent). The middle class (23 percent) and poor (13 percent) appear to have experienced more stress in their lives. Social class was self –identified as 'upper' or 'upper-middle, middle or lower-middle, and lower or lower-middle. The largest strata identified themselves as middle classes, 52 percent as contrasted with 21 percent upper classes, and 27 percent as lower classes in the Pew study.

The American Dream while still alive is not as strong as in past years. The American Dream was first publicly defined in 1931 by James Truslow Adams in Epic of America. Adam's often-repeated quote is, "The American Dream (is) that dream of a land in which life should be better and richer and fuller for every man, with opportunity for each according to his ability or achievement"

(Adams 1931, 404). A version of the American Dream has been polled by the New York Times since 1983. The question the New York Times asked is: "Do you think it is still possible to start out poor in this country, work hard, and become rich?" (New York Times/CBS Poll, 2014). Although the economy has improved since the 2008 recession, in 2014 the public is more pessimistic than before the financial crisis. The New York/CBS 2014 poll found that only 64 percent of the respondents said they still believed in the American Dream. While the percentage has fluctuated over time (see Table 2) this result is the lowest in two decades.

Another New York Times/CBS poll (2009) question, asked between 2005 and 2009, tapped another aspect of the American Dream. Parents were asked if they thought their children would be better, somewhat better, about the same, somewhat worse or much worse off than the parents at a similar age. Only 19 percent of parents believed their children's standard of living would be 'much better' in 2009, down from 25 percent in 2005 (see Table 3).

Table 2.

Think possible to start poor with hard work become rich	Possible	Not possible
Year, month and date		
1983 1/6-19	57%	38%
1996 2/22-24	70%	27%
1996 3/20-21 CBS	78%	18%
1998 4/15-20 NYT	70%	29%
2000 2/6-10 CBS	84%	13%
2003 7/13-27	70%	27%
2005 3/9-14 NYT	80%	19%
2007 6/26-28 CBS	81%	18%
2009 4/1-5	72%	24%
2011 2/24-27	82%	15%
2011 10/19-24	75%	24%
2012 7/11-16	71%	27%
2014 12/4-7 NYT	64%	33%

Source: New York Times/CBS Poll (2014).
Figures do not add up to 100%. Don't know not provided.

Table 3.

Little optimism for next generation	Worse off	Better off
Asia	24%	58%
Africa	27%	51%
Latin America	37%	50%
Middle East	41%	35%
United States	65%	25%
Europe Median percentages by region	65%	25%

Source: Pew Research Center Global Trends (2014).

Americans in 2014 were divided as to whether the economic system in the United States was basically fair (52 percent), allowing all Americans to have an equal opportunity to succeed, or basically unfair (45 percent) (New York Times/CBS Poll 2014).

OPTIMAL WEALTH

How do Americans see the optimal level of wealth inequality? What economic distribution is the ideal one? In a novel representative poll Americans were given a choice of three possible unlabeled pie charts (Norton and Ariely 2011). The first pie unlabeled pie chart provided equal wealth to each quintile of the population, 20 percent. The second pie chart showed the actual division of wealth in the United States, the top quintile owns 84 percent of the total wealth, the second quintile 11 percent, the third quintile 4 percent, and the bottom two quintiles less than 1 percent of the total wealth in the United States. The third pie chart illustrated the actual distribution of wealth according to quintiles in Sweden, the top quintile owns 18 percent of the wealth, the second quintile 38 percent, the third quintile 15 percent, the fourth quintile 21 percent of the wealth and the bottom quintile, 11 percent of the total wealth of the country.

Using Rawls' constraint (1971) Americans were asked to select a nation they would rather join, considering they could end up anywhere in the distribution from the richest to the poorest. There was an overwhelming preference for the Swedish distribution over the American distribution by 92 percent. The United States distribution was found by the respondents to be less desirable than both the Swedish distribution and the equal distribution.

Americans prefer some inequality to perfect equality, but definitely not to the degree that is currently present in the United States.

In the same poll (Norton and Ariely 2011) Americans were asked to plot the estimated and ideal wealth distribution of each quintile of the population in the United States. Respondents vastly underestimated the actual percentage of wealth concentration in the United States. Their ideal distribution was more equitable than their estimate of the top quintile (about 58 percent). The respondents preferred the top quintile to possess about 32 percent of the wealth. Women and those earning less $50,000 favored a slightly more equitable distribution of wealth.

GLOBAL ATTITUDES ON OPPORTUNITY AND INEQUALITY

How different are Americans in comparison to other advanced, emerging and developing countries in their hope for future generations? To what extent do individuals from different countries believe that success is determined by factors outside their control? Osberg and Smeeding (2006) found that attitudes on inequality in the U.S. are similar to other countries. However in a 1999 analysis of the International Social Survey Program (ISSP) they discovered that Americans in contrast to Norwegians, who on the average were in favor of significantly reducing the income gap, that the United States had a very polarized attitudinal picture. The United States had a significant number of respondents who favored more equality and a large group who agreed with the status quo (Osberg and Smeeding 2006). Inequality since the turn of the century has increased substantially.

A decade later Pew Research Center, Global Trends (2014) surveyed 44 countries from March 17 to June 5, 2014 to understand their beliefs on social mobility for their children. The countries were divided into three major categories: advanced economies (10 countries), emerging markets (25 countries) and developing economies (9 countries). The effect of the Great Recession, rapidly changing labor markets and globalization has produced less optimism in advanced countries than in emerging markets and developing countries. When asked "When children in our country grow up, will they be 'worse off' or 'better off' financially than their parents?" Advanced economies were less optimistic (65 percent worse off and 28 percent better off) than emerging markets (25 percent worse off and 50 better off) and developing economies (39 worse off and 51 better off).

Table 3 chronicles answers according to geographical area. Asians are particularly optimistic about the next generation's financial progress – 94 percent of Vietnamese, 85 percent of Chinese, 71 percent of Bangladeshis, and 67 percent of Indians believe their children will be better off than their parents. Once again one sees that the U.S. and Europe are the most pessimistic with Latin America and the Middle East in a middle ground.

Most individuals see inequality growing between rich and poor. There is more agreement on the gap between the rich and poor according to the Pew Social and Democratic Trends study (2014) than optimism than about their children's future. The advanced economies, emerging markets and developing economies median fell between above 56 and 60 percent in answering that there was growing gap between rich and poor. Among advanced countries Germany (39 percent) and Japan (28 percent) were least likely to view the gap between rich and poor as a big problem. Among emerging markets Vietnam (34 percent) and developing economies Bangladesh (34 percent) were least likely to see inequality as a major challenge.

Table 4.

Agree/Disagree success in life is pretty much determined by forces outside our control	Agree	Disagree
US	40%	57%
France	50%	50%
Germany	67%	31%
Greece	62%	37%
Italy	66%	32%
Poland	63%	34%
Spain	65%	26%
UK	43%	55%
Russia	50%	41%
Ukraine	59%	29%
China	58%	33%

Source: Pew Research Center Global Trends (2014).
Figures do not add up to 100%. Don't know/No Answer not provided.

Americans stand out from other countries with respect to individualism. This is associated with American exceptionalism. Lipset (1997) asserts that

American exceptionalism includes competitive individualism and self-determination. This is evident from the Pew Global Trends (2014) poll. Fifty-seven percent of Americans disagree with the statement "Success in life is pretty much determined by forces outside our control" in comparison with the global median of 38 percent (see Table 4). Americans also place a very strong emphasis on hard work to get ahead, 73 percent agree in comparison with a global median of 50 percent. The United Kingdom is closest to the US with 60 percent agreement that hard work is very important for upward mobility.

Paradoxes of Inequality and Welfare State Programs in the United States

Why do individuals vote against their interests to reduce welfare state programs? The part of the country that depends on safety-net programs, primarily supported by Democrats is increasing voting for anti-welfare Republicans. Several trends and theories help explain the paradox of inequality and growing conservatism in a large part of the United States. Luttig (2013) concludes in an analysis of Americans' attitudes toward redistribution of income that despite the fact that the United States is the most unequal of the advanced industrialized democracies, both the absolute level and the changing structure of inequality have been a force in promoting conservatism, not supporting redistribution as he theoretically expected.

Part of the swing toward conservatism among states where many individuals reply on safety net programs is related to voting. In a Pew Research Center study of nonvoters (2014) it found that nearly half of nonvoters (46 percent) have family incomes less than $30,000, compared with 19 percent of likely voters. Most nonvoters (54 percent) have not attended college in comparison with 72 percent of likely voters who have at least some college. Nonvoters are also much more likely to receive a means-tested government benefits in the last 12 months (33 percent) in contrast to likely voters (18 percent). Nonvoters are also less likely than voters to affiliate with a party. A similar result was reported by File (2015) for federal congressional elections. For those with annual incomes under $10,000 only 25 percent voted in comparison with individuals with family incomes of $150,000 and more, who voted over than twice the rate, (57 percent) in congressional elections in 2014.

The diminishing power of unions in the past four decades has played a powerful role in rising inequality. Rosenfeld (2014) argues that unions were the main equalizing institution in the U.S. following World War II. Unions, particularly in the private sector were important in the expansion of equality and the growth of the middle class. The subsequent weakening of unions has contributed to the stagnation of the middle class and increasing income inequality. Middle-income Americans have fallen further behind in the new century according to Pew 2014 findings (Pew Research Center Demographic Trends 2015). In 2014 the median income of these households was 4 percent less than 2000. The total income accruing to middle-income families was 43 percent in 2014, a substantial decline from 62 percent in 1970. Rosenfeld (2014) also observes that the decline in private sector unions has had an important effect on voting behavior and civic participation. Unions used to mobilize workers to vote, but they are less able to do that today.

The change from a manufacturing to a service economy has changed political alliances as well. There is now a weaker connection between labor and the Democratic Party. Halpern-Meekin, Edin and associates (2015) found a tendency by Americans in the second lowest quintile of the income ladder — the working or lower-middle class — to dissociate themselves from those at the bottom. Many white Americans turned against spending on welfare programs during the 1970s because they believed that they primarily served blacks (Wilson 1997).

One major reason that Americans distribute less to the poor than Europeans is that the majority of Americans believe that redistribution favors racial minorities (Alesina, Glaeser and Sacerdote 2001). In Fighting Poverty in the U.S. and Europe, Alesina and Glaeser (2006) concluded that about half of the gap between Europe and the United States in public spending could be explained by America's more varied racial and ethnic diversity. As indicated in Table 4, Americans believe that if someone is poor they are more likely to believe it is their own doing then Europeans.

Gilens (1999) argues that media in the United States exaggerates the relationship between minority status and poverty by over-representing people of color, particularly African Americans in news stories about poverty. In his analysis of national survey data, stereotyping blacks as lazy and the poor as undeserving emerged as the strongest predictor of white opposition to welfare, followed by individualism and conservatism.

PARTISAN DIVIDE AND NO CONSENSUS ON SOLUTIONS TO INEQUALITY AND POVERTY

Since 1987 – and particularly over the second decade of the century – the country has experienced a stark increase in partisan polarization. Across 48 different questions covering values about government, foreign policy, social and economic issues and other realms the average difference between the opinions of Republicans and Democrats increased significantly. In 2014 it stood at 18 percentage points. This is almost twice the size of the gap in surveys conducted from 1987-2002 (Pew Research Center, Numbers, Facts and Trends 2014).

Table 5.

How much should government do to reduce gap between rich and everyone else?	Republicans	Democrats
A lot/ some	45%	90%
Not/much	48%	10%
What would do more to reduce poverty?		
Raise taxes on wealthy and corporations	29%	75%
Lower taxes on wealthy and corporations	59%	17%
Government aid to the poor		
Does more good than harm	28%	66%
Does more harm than good	65%	26%

Source: Pew Research Center, Numbers, Facts and Trends (2014).

Table 5 analyzes attitudes toward inequality and attitudes toward the poor. The partisan gap between Democrats and Republicans spans a wide range of beliefs of the role of government. While Democrats believe strongly in the role of the federal government in reducing poverty and increasing taxes on the rich, the Republicans are opposed to these measures. The opposition intensifies when one asks about specific policies. Almost 40 percent more Republicans than Democrats believe that aid to the poor does more harm than good. Democrats have always been more committed than Republicans to government responsibilities in providing a social safety net and decreasing inequality through measures such a progressive tax policy. However, in both of those areas the divide between Democrats and Republicans has widened with an increasing divide between the values of the two major parties.

Bartels (2009) in Unequal America using extensive data spanning six decades shows the gap between the rich and poor has increased greatly under Republican administrations and decreased slightly under Democrats, leaving America grossly unequal.

He asserts that this is not simply the result of economic forces, but the product of broad-reaching policy choices in a political system dominated by partisan ideologies and the interests of the wealthy. Bartels found that elected officials respond to the views of affluent constituents but tend to disregard the views of poor people. As we have seen poor constituents are far less likely to vote in elections but more likely to receive mean-tested benefits.

CONCLUSION

Groups hold very different views based on class and race and ethnicity, gender and political ideology. This suggests why the debate on poverty and inequality is so intractable in the United States. Both sides believe in the justice of their irreconcilable positions. This is particularly true of the attitudes of partisans of the two parties. Republicans and Democrats have drifted further apart on their attitudes toward inequality and aid to the poor.

The dominant ideological context in which Republicans view inequality and the poor emphasizes individualism and meritocracy. They minimalize the tendency to see poverty as a personal problem related to circumstances in which the government should intervene. On the other hand, Democrats believe that poverty and inequality are primarily related to circumstances and not lack of effort so they support government invention to reduce inequality and poverty. This is underscored by several opinion polls. Quantitative research offers insight into how acceptance of economic inequality and poverty is driven by beliefs.

The evidence of this paper is in agreement with Osberg and Smeeding (2006, 470). They conclude that the "United States appears to be a country with much more polarization of attitudes toward income leveling than is common elsewhere, and increasingly over time." In the United States this polarization represents a partisan and racial divide.

While individuals are more likely to identify with their position in the class structure (Curtis and Anderson 2015) this does not completely explain the racial coding of poverty in the United States and sharp disagreements between the parties on government action. The stagnation of the middle classes and widening inequality has reduced the belief in the American dream, a belief that is central to our national identity. This has turned many white respondents against federal government intervention to reduce poverty and the rising income gap.

If there is a possibility of consensus between Republicans and Democrats and racial and ethnic minorities in the United States it appears to be in policies such as support for raising the minimum wage. According to a recent Pew 2014 poll (Five Facts about the Minimum Wage) overall 73 percent of the population favored an increase in the federal minimum wage from $7.25 to $10.10. A majority of Democrats (90 percent) and independents (71 percent) favored the increase as well as a slight majority of Republicans (53 percent).

What do our findings imply for Americans' views about fairness, opportunity and government activism? While many Americans have become concerned about inequality, a significant number of Americans are dissatisfied with assistance to the poor and with higher taxes on the rich. Republican beliefs about wealth support the perception that class position is based on merit. Attributions of poverty are correlated with a constellation of beliefs emphasizing personal responsibility. Democrats and racial and ethnic minorities, on the other hand strongly endorse government programs to reduce poverty and taxing the wealthy to reduce the income gap.

Primarily because of this large divide few new programs have been instituted to reduce poverty and counter rising inequality. If attitudes remain divided this is likely to continue to be the case. The actions that a majority of Americans have endorsed have tended to favor nontraditional redistributive programs such as the increase in minimum wage. A rise in funding for higher education for needy students if carefully crafted as related to merit is also a policy that may find the support of most Americans. Programs that emphasize equality of opportunity rather programs targeted toward the poor have a better chance of being instituted.

We have shown that a stark divide in opinion on government action to address poverty and inequality has impeded solutions in the United States. This is the case in spite of the fact that the US has the largest gap between rich and poor among the industrialized democracies. While Americans have become increasingly concerned about inequality and the realization of the American Dream, attitudes related to potential solutions to poverty and inequality remain decidedly divided.

REFERENCES

Adams, J. T. (1931). *The Epic of America*. Boston: Little, Brown.

Alesina, A., Glaeser, E. & Sacerdote, B. (2001). "Why doesn't the US have a European-Style Welfare State *Harvard Institute of Economic Research*. Discussion Paper 1933. November. Cambridge: Harvard University.

Alesina, A., Glaeser, E. (2006). *Fighting Poverty in the US and Europe*. New York: Oxford University Press.

Bartels, L. M. (2009). *Unequal America*. Princeton, NJ: Princeton University Press.

Curtis, J. & Andersen, R. (2015). "How Social Class shapes Attitudes on Economic Inequality: The Competing Forces of Self-Interest and Legitimation. *International Review of Social Research* 5, 4 - 19.

Feagin, J. R. (1975). *Subordinating the Poor: Welfare and American Beliefs*. Engelwood Cliffs, NJ: Prentice Hall.

File, T. (2015). "Who Votes? Congressional Elections and the American Electorate: 1978-2014." Population Characteristics. P20-577. Washington, DC: U.S. Census Bureau.

Fitzgerald, F. S. (1989). "The Rich Boy" In M. J. Bruccoli (Ed.), *The Short Stories of F. Scott Fitzgerald: A New Collection*, 317-349. New York: Charles Scribner's Sons,

Fry, R. & Kochhar, R. (2014). "America's wealth gap between middle-income and upper-income families is widest on record." *Pew Research Center*. December 17.

Gilens, M. (1999). *Why Americans Hate Welfare: Race, Media, and the Politics of Antipoverty Policy*. Chicago: University of Chicago Press.

Grusky, D. B. & MacLean, A. (2016). "The Social Fallout of a High-Equality Regime." *Annals of the American Academy of Political and Social Science* January, 33-52.

Halpern-Meekin, S., Edin, K., Tach, L., & Sykes, J. (2015). *How Working Families Make Ends Meet in a Post-Welfare World*. Berkeley: University of California Press.

Lipset, S. (1997). American Exceptionism: *A Double-Edged Sword*. New York: Norton.

Luttig, M. (2013). “The Structure of Inequality and Americans’ Attitudes toward Redistribution.” *Public Opinion Quarterly* 77, 811-821.

New York Times/CBS Poll. (2009). April 1-5. http://graphics8. nytimes.com/packages/pdf/national/20090507_american_dream_poll.pdf.

New York Times/CBS Poll. (2014). December 4-7. http://www.nytimes.com/interactive/2014/12/10/business/dealbook/document-poll-finds-a-more-bleak-view-of-american-dream.html.

Osberg, L. & Smeeding, T. (2006). “Fair” Inequality? Attitudes toward Pay Differentials: The United States in Comparative Perspective.” *American Sociological Review* 71, 450-473.

Pew Research Center, Demographic Trends (2015). “The Middle Class is Losing Ground. December. http://www.pewsocialtrends.org/files/2015/12/2015-12-09_middle-class_FINAL-report.pdf.

Pew Research Center, Facts and Trends. (2014). “The Party of Nonvoters.” October. http://www.people-press.org/files/2014/10/10-31-14-Party-of-Nonvoters-release.pdf.

Pew Research Center, Five Facts about the Minimum Wage. (2015). July. http://www.pewresearch.org/fact-tank/2015/07/23/5-facts-about-the-minimum-wage/

Pew Research Center, Global Trends. (2014). “Emerging and Developing Economies more Optimistic than Rich Countries about the Future.” October 9. http://www.pewglobal.org/files/2014/10/Pew-Research-Center-Inequality-Report-FINAL-October-9-2014.pdf.

Pew Research Center, Numbers, Facts and Trends. (2014). “Most see Inequality Growing, but Partisans differ over Solutions. January. http://www.people-press.org/files/legacy-pdf/1-23-14%20Poverty_Inequality%20Release.pdf.

Pew Research Center, Social and Demographic Trends. (2012). “Yes, the Rich are Different.” August 27. http://www.pewsocialtrends.org/files/2012/08/sdt-rich-poor-082712.pdf.

Pew Research Center. (2013). Americans see growing gap between rich and poor. December 5. http://www.pewresearch.org/fact-tank/2013/12/05/americans-see-growing-gap-between-rich-and-poor/.

Pew Social and Democratic Trends. (2012). “Rising Share of Americans see Conflict between Rich and Poor.” January 11. http://www.pewsocialtrends.org/files/2013/01/Rich_vs_poor-final_1-10-13.pdf.

Rawls, J. (1971). *A Theory of Justice*. Cambridge, MA: Harvard University Press.

Rosenfeld, J. (2014). *What Unions No Longer Do*. Cambridge, MA: Harvard University Press.

Saez, E. (2013). "Striking it richer: The evolution of top incomes in the United States. *Real-World Economics Review* 65, 120-128.

Saez, Emmanuel & Zucman, G. (2014). Wealth Inequality in the United States since 1913: Evidence from capitalized income tax data. NBER Working Paper 20625. Cambridge, MA.

Wilson, W. J. (1997). *When Work Disappears: The World of the New Urban Poor*. New York: Alfred Knopf.

In: Socioeconomic Status
Editor: Geoffrey Perkins

ISBN: 978-1-63485-326-2

Chapter 5

BENEFITS AND PITFALLS OF HIGH SOCIOECONOMIC STATUS BASED ON THREE FINDINGS IN JAPANESE SAMPLES

Ken'ichiro Nakashima[1,*] and Sumin Lee[2]

[1]Hiroshima University, Graduate School of Education, Hiroshima, Japan
[1]Hiroshima University, Faculty of Education, Hiroshima, Japan

ABSTRACT

Both folk wisdom and previous research have shown the benefits of high SES. For example, individuals of high SES consistently experience less morbidity and mortality from a variety of mental illnesses (Dohrenwend et al., 1992; Johnson, Cohen, Dohrenwend, Link, & Brook, 1999). High SES is also linked to an advantage across a variety of diseases, regardless of prevalence, severity, or mortality rates (Adler et al., 1994; Chen, Matthews, & Boyce, 2002). Moreover, Adler, Epel, Castellazzo, and Ickovics (2000) found that subjective SES was more positively related to psychological functioning and health-related factors than were more objective measures of SES. These findings were consistent with Chen and Paterson (2006).

---

* Corresponding author: Ken'ichiro Nakashima, Hiroshima University, Graduate School of Education, 1-1, Kagamiyama 1-chome, Higashi-Hiroshima, 739-8524, Japan. E-mail: kennakashi@hiroshima-u.ac.jp, Tel: +81-82-424-6772. This research was supported by the grant funding from the Mazda Foundation in Japan.

Although some previous works suggested the benefits of high SES, regardless of subjective or objective indicators, other researchers noted the pitfalls of high SES (for a review, see Kraus, Piff, & Keltner, 2011). Recent empirical research reported a positive relationship between SES and less prosocial behavior (Piff et al., 2010). In other research, individuals with lower SES were more engaged with others (Kraus & Keltner, 2009), more accurate at identifying the different emotions of others (Kraus et al., 2010), and showed more prosocial behavior (Piff et al., 2010) than individuals with higher SES. For example, in Piff's research, individuals reporting lower SES gave more monetary points to their anonymous partner than did high-SES participants. Taken together, it seems that high SES is related to benefits for mental and physical health, but also drawbacks for interpersonal relationships.

In this chapter, the authors introduce three different studies; one published and two unpublished. These findings underpin the proposal of the benefits and pitfalls of high SES from the different perspectives of previous research. The first study by Nakashima and Yanagisawa (2015) involved a questionnaire and an experimental study with female undergraduates. These focused on subjective SES and departmental identity, which interacted to reduce depressive tendencies and negative affective responding. In other words, individuals with higher subjective SES gain more benefits from group identity. In the second study with female undergraduates, an experimental study that focused on empathic accuracy to excluded others was conducted. Participants watched stimulus movies (an exclusion and an exclusion situation for a target), and speculated on the target's feelings in each situation. Results showed that low-SES participants more accurately identified the target's negative feelings and psychological pain than did high-SES participants, which implied negative effects of high-SES on interpersonal relationships. The final study used a questionnaire survey to verify the effectiveness of the shift-persist strategy. Previous research found that, even if individuals are in a low-SES environment, shifting oneself (accepting stress for what it is and adapting the self through reappraisals) in combination with persisting (enduring life with strength by holding on to meaning and optimism) buffers the adverse effects of low SES (Chen & Miller, 2012; Chen et al., 2015). The authors created the Japanese version of the shift-and-persist measure and examined whether subjective SES and shift-and-persist strategy interact to predict undergraduates' depression and psychological functioning. Through the findings of these three studies, future directions for SES research were discussed.

INTRODUCTION

The human being is a "social animal." For humans, being in interpersonal relationships or, broadly-speaking, social systems, is not only given but essential. Considering that a social system is underpinned by differences of social power or economic resources, which are termed socioeconomic status, it is important to explore how these differences affect us for the purpose of understanding humans who live in social systems. In this chapter, the authors thus introduce three different studies, one published and two unpublished, underpinning the proposal of the benefits and pitfalls of high SES from the different perspectives of previous research. Through the findings of these three studies, we discuss future directions for SES research.

Socioeconomic status (SES) is defined as material wealth, occupation, and participation in educational and social institutions (Oakes & Rossi, 2003). Therefore, SES can be measured objectively in terms of family income and educational attainment; that is, so-called objective SES (Lachman & Weaver, 1998). In earlier research, SES is related to risk of disease and premature death (e.g., Adler, Marmot, McEwen, & Stewart, 1999; Kaye, Folsom, Prineas, Potter, & Gapstur, 1990). Moreover, evidence is stronger for SES effects on health, although some of the association may be derived from health effects on SES (e.g., Fox, Goldblatt, & Jones, 1985; Haan, Kaplan, & Syme, 1989). In recent research, objective SES has been positively related to subjective SES, which, in turn, contributed to increased individual self-esteem (Kraus & Park, 2014).

Turning to previous studies focused on educational attainment as one indicator of SES, people who are more highly educated have better job opportunities, greater labor force flexibility, are less likely to be affected by unemployment trends, live longer and healthier lives, and, ultimately, receive higher salaries and lifetime earnings (Oreopoulos & Salvanes 2011). In addition, Nikolaev and Rusakov (2015) showed that educated people, on average, are happier than their less-educated counterparts starting in their early to mid-30s, and the happiness differential starts growing in favor of the more highly educated beyond this age. This pattern implies two points. First, a typical person in their 40s who has engaged in education beyond high school would be happier than a person of a similar socioeconomic background who has only completed high school or lower education. Second, this happiness gap increases with age; largely because the happiness trajectory of someone with high-school (or lower) education is predicted to be downward over the course of his or her life (Nikolaev & Rusakov, 2015). Other research showed that, based on findings from the 1958 British birth cohort, early negative circumstances that are mainly derived from childhood SES could be associated with physiological wear-and-tear in midlife, as measured by allostatic load; that is, the overall physiological wear-and-tear over the life course. This implies that a biological link between adverse childhood exposures and adult health is plausible (Solís et al., 2015).

Although the previous research introduced here mainly focused on the effects of objective SES, there is other research that emphasizes the effects not of objective SES but of subjective SES. One of the most famous studies is Adler et al., (2000). Individuals possess a subjective sense of SES on the basis of objective indicators such as family income and educational attainment (Kraus, Piff, Mendoza-Denton, Rheinschmidt, & Keltner, 2012). Comparing the effects of objective SES with those of subjective SES, Adler et al., (2000) found that subjective SES was more strongly related to psychological functioning and health-related factors than objective measures of SES. For example, subjective SES, as measured on a ladder scale, was positively related to a sense of control over one's life and negatively related to pessimism. In a similar vein, Chen and Paterson (2006) showed that subjective SES was positively related to self-esteem and a sense of control, and Singh-Manoux, Marmot, and Adler (2005) showed that subjective SES continues to be significantly associated with health and changes in health after controlling for objective SES.

In sum, previous research seems to convey common knowledge of SES, though there were differences of focus (i.e., objective or subjective SES) or indicators of SES (e.g., education and salary) among them; namely, emphasis on the benefits of high SES. This also seems consistent with folk wisdom regarding SES, which is shared in laypeople. However, the authors differentiate themselves from folk wisdom. In other words, high SES gives us some benefits yet it takes away from us something that is needed as social animals. In what follows, we discuss the *yin and yang* of high SES, introducing relevant findings.

On this point, the findings of previous research were informative. For example, Piff et al., (2010) showed that, across three experimental studies and one online questionnaire survey, lower SES individuals proved to be more generous, charitable, trusting, and helpful compared with their upper SES counterparts. Relatedly, national survey research indicated that high-income people spend a larger portion of their income on costly consumer goods (e.g., automobiles) and disproportionately less on assisting others in need (Frank, 1999). Dubois, Rucker, and Galinsky (2015) pointed out that high SES individuals behaved unethically for the purpose of self-interest. Moreover, based on previous findings that low SES individuals favor explanations of personal and political outcomes that are oriented to features of the external environment (Kraus, Piff, & Keltner, 2009), Kraus, Côté, and Keltner (2010) demonstrated that individuals of low SES were more empathically accurate in judging other people's emotions. In other words, low SES led us to empathic accuracy. Considering that prosocial behaviors or empathic accuracy could lead to good interpersonal relationships, it is plausible that high SES has advantages and disadvantages. In other words, low SES seems to not always be harmful to individuals.

In this chapter, we introduce three different studies. These findings underpin the proposal of the benefits and pitfalls of high SES from the different perspectives of previous research. The first study by Nakashima and Yanagisawa (2015) involved a questionnaire study and an experimental study with female undergraduates. These focused on subjective SES and departmental identity, which interacted to reduce depressive tendencies and negative affective responding. In the second study with female undergraduates, focusing on empathic accuracy to excluded others, low SES participants more accurately identified the target's negative feelings and psychological pain than did high SES participants. The final study used a questionnaire survey to verify the effectiveness of the shift-persist strategy. The authors created the Japanese version of the shift-and-persist measure and examined whether subjective SES and shift-and-persist strategy interact to predict undergraduates' depression and psychological functioning. In the latter section, we introduce each study in more detail.

Socioeconomic Status and Departmental Identity Interact to Reduce Depressive Tendencies and Negative Affective Responding for Female Undergraduates (Study 1)

How do SES and departmental identity promote the mental health of female undergraduates? Focusing not on objective SES but on subjective SES, Nakashima and Yanagisawa (2015) conducted a questionnaire study (Study 1) and an experimental study (Study 2) with undergraduates enrolled in a women's junior college to examine whether SES and departmental identity have an interactive effect on mental health. In this section, we introduce a brief report of each study.

Departmental identity is one type of group identity and is an aspect of self-concept that is derived from perceived membership in the departments to which undergraduates belong. Departmental identity seems to play the same roles as other types of group identity, considering previous findings that related group identity to belongingness, self-esteem, control, and meaningful existence (Smart Richman & Leary, 2009; Williams, 2007). Relatedly, expected social support derived from departmental identity not only causes undergraduates to underestimate potential threats in stressful situations but also leads them to lower their depression tendency (Nakashima, Isobe, & Ura, 2013). These findings have suggested that departmental identity plays a key role in an undergraduate's psychological functioning and mental health.

Nevertheless, it would be more difficult for undergraduates with low SES to obtain the benefits of departmental identity, which means improved psychological functioning and enhanced mental health, compared with undergraduates with high SES. This is because low SES undergraduates have a relatively vulnerable sense of departmental identity. In previous research, low SES undergraduates are sensitive to dissimilarities with other departmental members or to other members' responses to them (Johnson, Richeson, & Finkel, 2011; Kraus, Piff, Mendoza-Denton, Rheinschmidt, & Keltner, 2012). Other research suggested that SES was negatively related to undergraduates' concerns about discrimination based on one's social class (i.e., class-based rejection sensitivity), and their class-based rejection sensitivity was related to a low level of expected academic grades, as well as a high depressive tendency (Rheinschmidt & Mendoza-Denton, 2014). Therefore, low subjective SES undergraduates would obtain group-based benefits less easily than undergraduates with high subjective SES. In other words, high subjective SES undergraduates are likely to fully enjoy both SES-based and group-based benefits. In contrast, low subjective SES undergraduates manage to receive the benefits of departmental identity only when they are able to attain a stable sense of this identity. In sum, we predicted that, even if undergraduates belong to and identify with their department, it might be difficult for them to receive the psychological benefits of departmental identity unless they also have high subjective SES.

In the first study of Nakashima and Yanagisawa (2015), a nearly longitudinal questionnaire survey was conducted in order to provide initial evidence regarding an interactive effect of subjective SES and departmental identity on undergraduates' mental health. The participants were 61 undergraduates (average age = 19.49 years, *SD* = 1.34) enrolled in a women's junior college in western Japan. Participants evaluated their SES on the basis of social rank and family income. Participants were asked to indicate their social rank on a 10-point scale, from 1 (upper rank) to 10 (lower rank), and their family income scale using 7-point ratings from 1 (much less than average) to 7 (much greater than average). Moreover, participants assessed the extent to which they identified with their department using a modified version (Nakashima, Isobe, & Ura, 2012) of the group identification scale (Karasawa, 1991), in addition to their state of depressive tendency using the Todai Health Index (Suzuki et al., 1979), 3 months apart. We focused on the change in participants' group identity and depressive tendency in order to investigate the causal relationship among relevant variables. Regarding the interactive effect, we predicted that, even if participants have a high level of departmental identity, group-based benefits would decrease if they were low in subjective SES. In other words, a low level of depressive tendency derived from departmental identity would decrease in the case of low SES.

Table 1 presents the means, standard deviations, and correlations of the measures used in this study. Because social rank was positively related to family income, as shown in Table 1 and suggested by Kraus and Keltner (2009), scores for participants' social rank and family income were standardized and then averaged to create a composite measure of overall SES.

In order to examine our prediction, we first conducted two simple regression analyses. These analyses enabled us to generate participants' residual scores, which represented depressive tendency at Time 2, controlling for depressive tendency at Time 1. A high residual score therefore indicated an increase in depressive tendency. We chose the same approach to departmental identity. Next, we conducted a series of hierarchical multiple regressions of the residual score for depression tendency, as suggested by Aiken and West (1991). The predictors were participants' residual scores for departmental identity, overall SES, and the two-way interaction effects. Standardized departmental identity (residuals) and overall SES scores were entered into the equation at Step 1, and the two-way interaction values were entered at Step 2.

The results showed that the main effect of residual scores of departmental identity was significant: $b = -0.21$, $t(57) = -4.68$, $p < .001$. The increase of departmental identity was related to the decrease of depressive tendency. Importantly, the two-way interaction approached significance: $b = -0.10$, $t(57) = -2.37$, $p = .05$. The results of the simple slopes for overall SES (Figure 1) showed that, for high SES participants (+1 SD), residual depressive scores were negatively related to residual departmental identity scores, $b = -0.30$, $t(57) = -4.91$, $p < .001$, whereas, for low SES participants (−1 SD), this pattern approached significance: $b = -0.11$, $t(57) = -1.92$, $p = .06$.

Table 1. Variables assessed in Study 1: Means, standard deviations and zero-order correlations between variables

	M	*SD*	1	2	3	4	5	6	7
1. group identity (time1)	3.75	0.45	-	.62**	−.26*	−.05	−.20	−.08	−.17
2. group identity (time2)	3.76	0.57	-	-	−.12	−.36**	−.30*	−.09	−.24
3. depression (time1)	0.59	0.41	-	-	-	.44**	−.08	−.14	−.14
4. depression (time2)	0.59	0.44	-	-	-	-	−.12	.07	−.03
5. social rank	5.28	1.20	-	-	-	-	-	.34**	.82**
6. family income	3.43	1.19	-	-	-	-	-	-	.82**
7. overall SES	0.00	0.82	-	-	-	-	-	-	-

Note. * $p < .05$, ** $p < .01$

In addition, the results of the simple slopes for departmental identity showed that residual depression scores were negatively related to overall SES scores for high-identified participants (+1 SD), $b = -0.13$, $t(57) = -1.98$, $p = .05$. However, this pattern disappeared for low-identified participants (−1 SD), $b = 0.07$, $t(57) = 1.17$, ns.

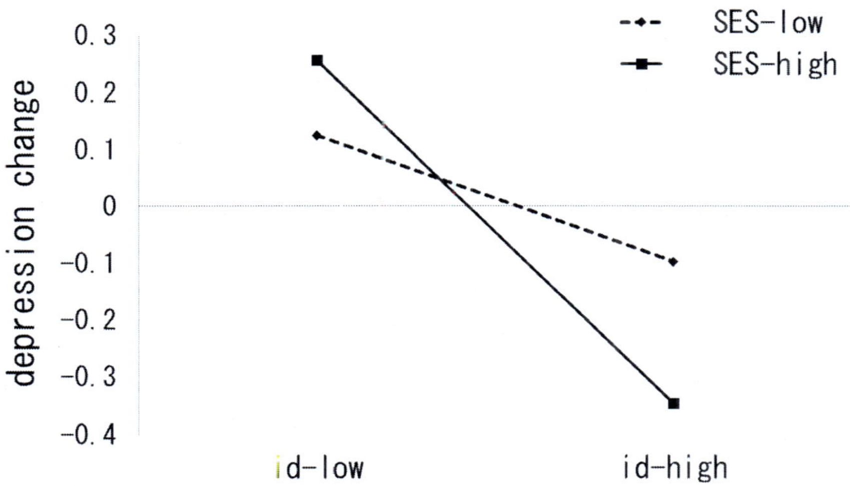

Figure 1. Depression change as a function of SES and departmental identity in the first study of Nakashima and Yanagisawa (2015, *Japanese psychological research*).

*Additional information in Figure 1

	id-low	id-high
SES-low	0.125	-0.097
SES-high	0.257	-0.347

Taken together, the series of results generally supported our prediction, suggesting that individuals with high SES and also identified with their departments had the lowest depressive tendency. Although previous studies found that, compared with objective SES, subjective SES more strongly predicted self-rated health and physiological health outcomes (Adler et al., 2000; Singh-Manoux et al., 2005), subjective SES and departmental identity do not benefit individuals independently. In other words, these factors work interactively to influence depression. As suggested in relevant research (Johnson et al., 2011; Kraus et al., 2012; Rheinschmidt & Mendoza-Denton, 2014), this background seems vulnerable in terms of departmental identity for low SES undergraduates: low SES undergraduates may have a more vulnerable sense of departmental identity than undergraduates with high SES, and, thus, low SES undergraduates may obtain group-based benefits less easily than undergraduates with high SES.

Based on the findings of the first study, Nakashima and Yanagisawa (2015) aimed to provide additional evidence regarding an interactive effect of SES and departmental identity on undergraduates' mental health. In the second study, we focused on the interactive effect arising in stressful situations. In previous research, a high level of subjective SES (Yanagisawa et al., 2013) and group identity (Knowles & Gardner, 2008) lowered individuals' need dissatisfaction or negative feelings, which were basically derived from social exclusion. Considering that need dissatisfaction or negative feelings were likely to cause maladaptive thoughts and behaviors (Nesdale & Lambert, 2007), it is important to examine whether the interactive effect arises in social exclusion situations.

In the second study of Nakashima and Yanagisawa (2015), both questionnaire and experimental sessions for female undergraduates were utilized. The experimental session focused on affective responding to a social exclusion situation, which manipulated a future-belonging or future-alone condition (Baumeister, DeWall, Ciarocco, & Twenge, 2005). The participants were 56 undergraduates (average age = 18.87 years, SD = 0.94) enrolled in a women's junior college in western Japan. In the questionnaire session, participants responded to the scales of subjective SES and departmental identity using similar measures to those of the first study, except for two additional scales. The first was the childhood SES scale (Griskevicius, Tybur, Delton, & Robertson, 2011), which measured the extent to which people experienced resource scarcity during childhood as a measure of subjective childhood SES. This addition aimed to cover the construct of SES more totally than the first study. The second was the independent-interdependent self-construal scale (Takata, 2000). This scale was used instead of the Eysenck Personality Questionnaire (EPQ; Eysenck & Eysenck, 1975), which has been used in previous research to manipulate a future-belonging or future-alone condition.

In an experimental session one week after the questionnaire session, social exclusion was manipulated by randomly assigning participants to receive bogus feedback about the future trajectory of their social lives (Baumeister et al., 2005). In the second study, we provided each participant with a false extraversion score based on the independent-interdependent self-construal scale, which seems to include items that ostensibly assess this construct. We then randomly assigned participants the conditions in the following experimental session. Therefore, we did not compute accurate scores on this self-construal scale. Participants in the crucial (future-alone) condition (N = 35) were told, ostensibly on the basis of their responses to the questionnaire, that they would likely end up alone in life. Participants in the future-belonging condition (N = 21) were told that they would likely spend the rest of their lives surrounded by people who cared about them. This manipulation of future belongingness was similar to that of previous research (e.g., Baumeister et al., 2005). After this manipulation of future belongingness, participants were asked to respond to affective scales of need dissatisfaction and negative feelings. These methods enabled us to uncover the causal relationship between subjective SES and departmental identity, and the negative effects of social exclusion.

Participants completed a questionnaire that assessed need dissatisfaction and negative feelings as main outcomes. We measured need dissatisfaction in response to social exclusion by using items based on the need satisfaction scale (Williams, 2009), each of which was rated on a 5-point scale. The items were selected because some items of Williams's scale were not appropriate for the experimental setting of the second study. We computed an index of need dissatisfaction so that the higher scores reflected higher need dissatisfaction. In addition, we measured the negative feelings scale in response to social exclusion using six items; each rated on a 5-point scale (Yanagisawa, 2011). We computed an index of negative feelings so that lower scores on this scale were taken to reflect positive feelings and higher scores to reflect negative feelings. Finally, as a control variable, participants responded to an item asking how much they doubted the feedback about their future belongingness (1 = do not doubt at all to 9 = doubt extremely).

The main purpose of this study was to examine if an interactive effect of subjective SES and departmental identity arose in a social exclusion situation but not in a social acceptance situation. In other words, we expected that the need dissatisfaction and negative feelings of higher-SES participants with higher departmental identity would be lessened in the future-alone condition. First, we conducted a series of hierarchical multiple regressions of need dissatisfaction for participants in the future-alone condition. The predictors were participants' departmental identity, overall SES, and the two-way interaction effects. The overall SES score was generated as in the first study, based on the patterns that subjective social rank was related to family income, $N = 35$, $r = .51$, $p = .002$, in addition to childhood SES, $r = .50$, $p = .002$, and family income was also related to childhood SES, $r = .60$, $p < .001$.

Multiple regression analysis showed not only the nearly-significant main effect of overall SES, $b = -0.18$, $t(31) = -2.03$, $p = .05$, but also the two-way interaction, $b = -0.21$, $t(31) = -1.74$, $p = .09$. Two significant relationships emerged in the test of simple slopes. For high-SES participants (+1 SD), need dissatisfaction scores were negatively related to departmental identity scores, $b = -0.32$, $t(31) = -2.27$, $p = .03$. For high-identified participants (+1 SD), need dissatisfaction scores were negatively related to overall SES scores, $b = -0.39$, $t(31) = -2.45$, $p = .02$. These results supported our prediction. In contrast, the two-way interaction did not emerge for participants' need dissatisfaction scores in the future-belonging condition, $N = 21$, $b = -0.10$, $t(17) = -1.03$, ns. These results supported our prediction.

Next, we conducted a series of hierarchical multiple regressions of negative feelings, adding standardized scores with the degree of doubt about the feedback for participants at Step 0 as a control variable in the equation. Similar to the case of need dissatisfaction, the two-way interaction was significant, $b = -0.35$, $t(30) = -2.32$, $p = .03$, as was the effect of doubt about feedback, $b = 0.26$, $t(30) = 2.31$, $p = .03$. In the test of the simple slopes, as depicted in Figure 2, for high-SES participants (+1 SD), negative feelings scores were negatively related to departmental identity scores, $b = -0.49$, $t(30) = -2.86$, $p = .008$. For high-identified participants (+1 SD), negative feelings scores were negatively related to overall SES scores, $b = -0.49$, $t(30) = -2.45$, $p = .02$. In contrast, the two-way interaction did not emerge for participants' negative feelings scores in the future-belonging condition, $b = -0.04$, $t(16) = -0.23$, ns. These results also supported our prediction in the case of need dissatisfaction.

In previous research, higher subjective SES and departmental identity led to effective coping in the social exclusion situation (Knowles & Gardner, 2008; Yanagisawa et al., 2013). However, these factors did not benefit individuals independently. In other words, subjective SES and departmental identity interacted to lessen undergraduates' responses of negative affect in the social exclusion situation. Considering the findings of both the first and second study, subjective SES and departmental identity jointly affect undergraduates' daily mental states, as well their negative-situation-specific responses, in a positive way. These findings were valuable in that there has been no previous investigation of the unique and interactive effects of subjective SES and departmental identity on mental health to our knowledge. As one aspect of future research, we should focus on other important reference groups in order to clarify the boundary conditions of our findings; in particular, organizational identity for employees. This is because it is not certain whether subjective SES and organizational identity interact to predict employees' mental health. If organizational identity would depend on objective SES based on a reference group, such as income or job position within an organization, there is the possibility of a positive but spurious relationship between organizational identity and subjective SES for employees. An objective SES effect may thus mask an interactive effect of subjective SES and organizational identity, because employees' objective SES may influence not only their subjective SES but also organizational identity. For us, this masking effect of objective SES deserves detailed consideration.

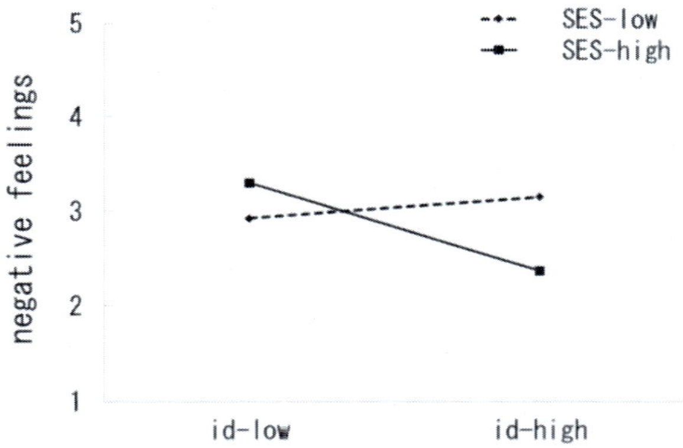

Figure 2. Negative feelings as a function of SES and departmental identity in future-alone condition in the second study of Nakashima and Yanagisawa (2015, *Japanese psychological research*).

*Additional information in Figure 2

	id-low	id-high
SES-low	2.924	3.152
SES-high	3.299	2.367

Low SES Leads Female Undergraduates to Empathic Accuracy of Psychological Pain for Excluded Classmates (Study 2; Unpublished Data)

The findings of Study 1 were consistent with previous studies reporting the benefits of high subjective SES (e.g., Adler et al., 2000; Singh-Manoux et al., 2005) in that it was difficult for female undergraduates with low subjective SES to receive the benefit from their departmental identity. However, the authors think that the simple structural outline of "high SES is good and low SES is bad" is too typical and therefore less interesting. Consistent with *yin and yang* in Chinese culture, there seem to be some pitfalls of high subjective SES.

In this regard, Kraus and colleagues provided some suggestive findings (e.g., Kraus & Keltner, 2009; Kraus et al., 2010; Piff et al., 2010). For example, Piff et al., (2010) hypothesized that lower SES individuals would show greater prosocial behavior because of their heightened concern for the welfare of others. This hypothesis is based on the idea that this concern is a means of adapting to their more hostile environments, and, subsequently, this orientation gives rise to greater prosocial behavior. Across three experimental studies and one online questionnaire survey, lower SES individuals proved to be more generous, charitable, trusting, and helpful compared with their upper SES counterparts. Moreover, in the analyses of mediating and moderating effects, a greater commitment to egalitarian values and feelings of compassion played an important role in the process whereby lower SES individuals acted in a more prosocial fashion. Relatedly, other research demonstrated the selfishness of high SES individuals. Dubois et al., (2015) proposed a key conceptual distinction between selfish and unethical behavior in order to address whether the rich are more unethical than the poor. Based on this distinction and employing six experiments, Dubois et al., (2015) showed that, although SES positively predicted unethical behavior, this relationship was only observed when that behavior was self-beneficial. That is, high SES individuals behave unethically for the purpose of self-interest. Moreover, high SE does not inherently lead to unethical behavior but instead predicts tendencies to behave selfishly. These findings suggest the pitfalls of high SES, along with a series of research by Kraus and colleagues.

In this section, the authors reported unpublished experimental data to expand the findings of SES and empathic accuracy (Kraus et al., 2010). Empathic accuracy reflects the ability to judge the emotions of other individuals (Ickes, Stinson, Bissonnette, & Garcia, 1990). Kraus et al., (2010) predicted that lower SES individuals would demonstrate higher levels of empathic accuracy than their higher counterparts based on two reasons. First, low SES individuals were more oriented to features of social context whereas high SES individuals tend to focus inward on their own unique qualities and characteristics. Additionally, low SES individuals should be sensitive to the emotions and actions of other people. In other words, low SES individuals have a "contextualism" tendency. Second, considering that empathic accuracy is needed and enhanced in interdependent relationships or societies (Stinson &

Ickes, 1992) and lower SES individuals were oriented to social engagement and interdependence as a means to adapt to their more hostile environments (Piff et al., 2010), it should also engender greater empathic accuracy among these individuals. Kraus et al., (2010) predicted that, as a result of these tendencies, low SES individuals would be more attentive to the emotions of others and judge these emotions more accurately than upper-class individuals. They found a parallel pattern of results across three experiments. In one study, high-school-educated participants (who were one example of low SES individuals) showed greater empathic accuracy—by more accurately decoding emotions displayed in static facial expressions—relative to college-educated participants (who were one example of high SES individuals). The same patterns emerged in an experimental setting that manipulated subjective social rank.

In Study 2, the authors focused on empathizers' empathic accuracy regarding the psychological pain of an excluded classmate in an interpersonal situation, and attempted to expand Kraus's findings from the two following perspectives. First, the authors relied on an experimental stimulus simulating everyday social interactions. Zaki and Ochsner (2009; 2012) pointed out the possibility that the researcher cannot elucidate how the empathizer puts the multiple social cues together (e.g., facial and bodily expressions, prosody, communication content, situational context, etc.), as individuals do in everyday social interactions, in many cases of neuroscience research. In an attempt to resolve the disaggregation between empathic process in an experimental setting and in everyday social interactions, a stimulus movie was very useful. The author thus used two stimulus movies that had been employed in a previous study (Nakashima, 2014). These movies consisted of an acceptance and an exclusion scene, each of which was approximately three minutes in length.

Second, in order to identify whether empathizers overestimate or underestimate the psychological pain of an excluded classmate, depending on empathizers' SES, the author focused on difference scores that subtracted genuine response of an excluded classmate from empathizers' estimation regarding the psychological pain of an excluded classmate by asking participants to respond to the same scales for an excluded classmate and empathizers. Were these scores zero, empathizers would show estimation most accurately. Were the value plus, it would mean that empathizers overestimate the psychological pain of an excluded classmate. Were it minus, it would mean underestimation. Considering that, in relevant research, absolute deviation scores (which reflect the degree to which a person's judgments of a target's absolute level of emotion match the absolute level of emotion that the target reports feeling) or profile correlations (which assess whether a person evaluates a target's level of emotion relative to other emotions) were used (see Côté et al., 2011; Fletcher & Kerr, 2010), our approach seems to be novel and informative, though challenging.

In Study 2, 76 undergraduate students (average age = 20.62 years, SD = 5.41) who were enrolled in an all-female junior college in western Japan participated in an experiment that consisted of a questionnaire session and an experimental session. In the questionnaire session, participants completed scales of SES similar to the second study in Nakashima and Yanagisawa (2015), expect for one scale of current/future SES used in Griskevicius et al., (2011). Along with the suggestions of Murayama (2012), the composite score of the four SES scales was determined by principal component analysis, with higher composite scores reflecting higher socioeconomic status.

One week after the questionnaire session, the experimental session was conducted. Due to the limited capacity of the room used for the group experiment, it was necessary to split the participants into two groups, with participants who belonged to the first group participating in a group experiment session, referred to as Class YA (n = 39), and the remaining participants (Class YB, n = 38) being subject to the same experimental condition some days later. As noted previously in this section, the focus of Study 2 was on empathic accuracy for the excluded classmates. Thus, two different sets of stimulus movies used in a previous study (Nakashima, 2014) were prepared for each group. For participants in Class YA, the central character (i.e., *A-San*) in the movie was a YA classmate, and, for participants in Class YB, the central character was a YB classmate. Other than the stimulus movies, there were no differences between YA and YB groups with respect to the experimental procedures.

In the experimental session, participants observed the stimulus movie of the acceptance scene and were asked to infer what *A-San* might have thought and felt during the scene. In acceptance scenes, the two genuine actors (*A-San* and the other) and the four confederates engage in the conversational game after the pre-briefing by the assistant. In this condition, the four confederates show their acceptance of the two actors by engaging them in a conversation. Prior to videotaping, the confederates had been instructed to accept *A-San* and the other actor in the conversation game. In the exclusion scene, after videotaping the conversation in the acceptance scene is done, the six persons vote on selecting three pairs for the next conversational game. This is done by the six members anonymously selecting their preferred partners for the next game. After tallying the votes, the assistant informed members of the result that the four confederates have been selected as the next two pairs. However, unknown to the two genuine actors, the outcome of the vote had been predetermined with the help of the confederates. Then, the four confederates also express their pleasure at having been paired with one another. The exclusion scene is then completed. In each condition, *A-San* completed the two same measures in the case of the participants, as noted below.

First, participants were administered two items regarding the estimated psychological pain of *A-San* in the acceptance scene. In order to measure estimated psychological pain, a Japanese version of the Faces Pain Scale (FPS) was used (Iimura et al., 2002). Participants were asked to choose the face that best corresponded with the intensity of psychological pain they estimated that *A-San* might have been experiencing in this scene. Next, participants were asked to watch the exclusion scene and to infer what *A-San* thought and felt in the scene. Participants were asked to complete the same item regarding estimated psychological pain. In addition, participants were asked to estimate how negatively *A-San* felt in the exclusion scene. In order to measure estimated negative feelings, participants completed a modified version of the Negative Feelings Scale (Yanagisawa, 2011), which was used in the second study of Nakashima and Yanagisawa (2015). Although participants completed other measures, this information is omitted here because of the purpose of Study 2.

Given that lower SES individuals were more accurate than higher SES individuals at perceiving the emotions that others experience, as shown in Kraus et al., (2010), the authors predicted that the empathic-accuracy scores of low SES would be closer to zero than those of high SES in the acceptance and exclusion situation for a classmate. Moreover, considering that lower SES individuals were oriented to social engagement and interdependence as a means of adapting to their more hostile environments (Piff et al., 2010), their tendency would be intensified in the exclusion situation, which is an interpersonal-difficulty condition for a classmate. In other words, the relationship between SES and empathic-accuracy in the exclusion situation would be stronger than in the acceptance situation. In order to examine this prediction, the authors conducted a simple regression analysis of the participants' empathic-accuracy scores in each acceptance and exclusion situation. The predictors were the composite score of the four SES scales. As noted previously, participants' empathic-accuracy scores were created by subtracting the genuine response of an excluded classmate (e.g., *A-San*) from their estimation regarding the psychological pain of an excluded classmate.

Consistent with our prediction, participants' empathic-accuracy scores of psychological pain in the exclusion situation were positively related to their SES composite scores ($b = 0.39$, $t(74)=2.52$, $p = .01$), whereas their empathic-accuracy scores in the acceptance situation were not related to their SES scores ($b = 0.10$, $t(74) = 0.80$, *ns.*). As depicted in Figure 3, their scores of low SES were closer to zero than those of high SES in the exclusion situation, suggesting overestimation of high SES individuals regarding the psychological pain of an excluded classmate. In the case of estimated negative feelings, the same patterns emerged as depicted in Figure 4 ($b=0.15$, $t(74) = 2.01$, $p < .05$), suggesting overestimation of high SES individuals.

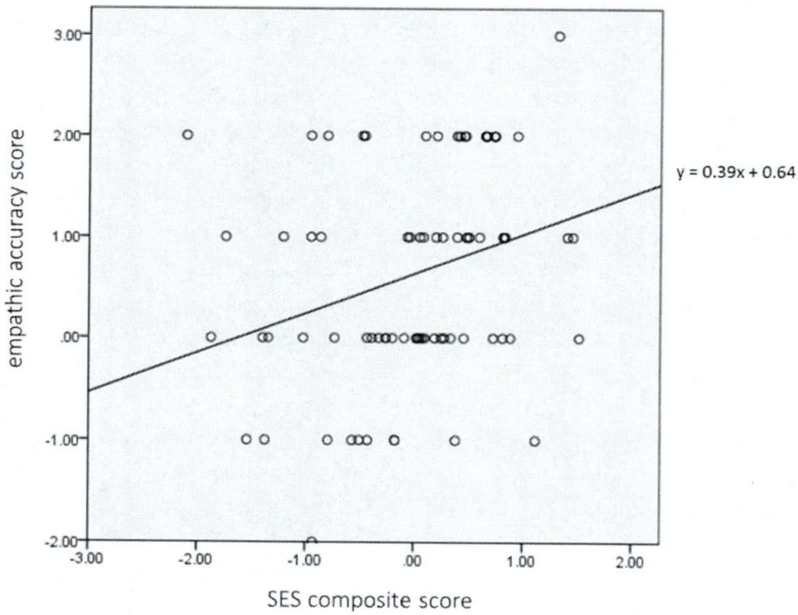

Figure 3. The relationship between SES and empathic accuracy of psychological pain in the exclusion situation.

The results introduced in Study 2 provided us with two implications. First, the findings of Kraus and colleagues were replicated in an experimental setting using a stimulus movie simulating everyday social interactions, suggesting that the causal relationship of low SES leading to high empathic accuracy is robust. Notably, it is suggestive that this relationship arose not in an acceptance situation for a classmate but in an exclusion situation. As noted above, since lower SES individuals were oriented to social engagement and interdependence as a means of adapting to their more hostile environments (Piff et al., 2010), lower SES individuals may be more sensitive to the adversity of surrounding others (i.e., social exclusion), which is a potential threat to themselves. In other words, for lower SES individuals, empathic accuracy seems to be key to attaining both their welfare and surrounding others' welfare.

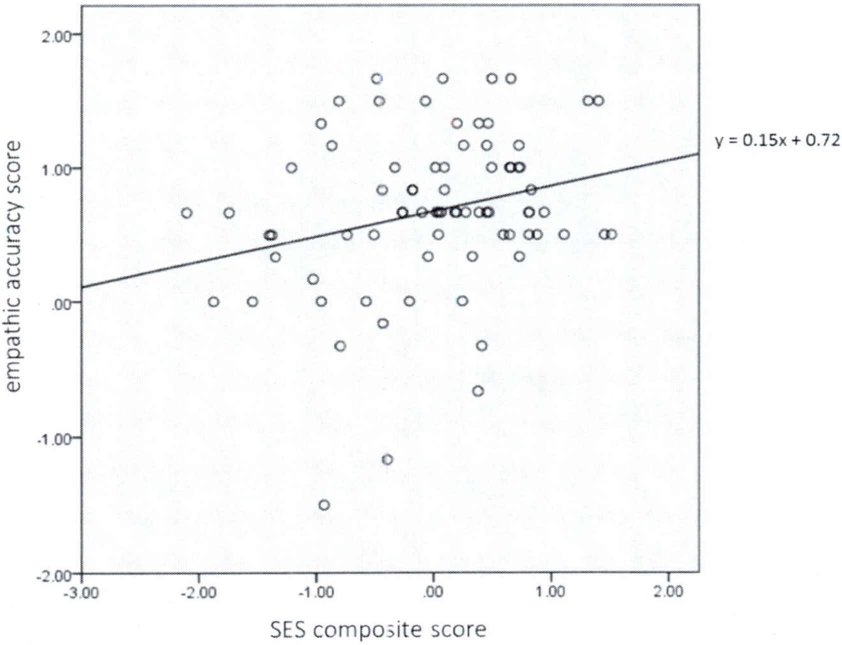

Figure 4. The relationship between SES and empathic accuracy of negative feelings in the exclusion situation.

Second, by using difference scores that subtracted genuine response of an excluded classmate from empathizers' estimation regarding psychological pain of an excluded classmate, we found a tendency of empathic inaccuracy for high SES individuals: an overestimation of psychological pain and negative feelings. Moreover, this tendency was reflected by a linear relationship between SES composite scores and empathic accuracy scores. In other words, the higher the SES, the greater the inaccuracy of judging others' psychological pain. Considering that empathic accuracy reflects the ability to judge the emotions of other individuals (Ickes et al., 1990) and is an important predictor of relationship outcomes and social adjustment (Côté & Miners, 2006), individuals in a high SES environment seem to lose an important aspect of the "human as a social animal" instead of benefitting from high SES.

The authors think that the key to resolving this problem is the activation of contextualism for high SES individuals. Kraus et al., (2010) revealed that contextual explanations involved a property tied to a particular time or place that mediated the relationship between subjective social rank and empathic accuracy. In this study, subjective social rank was measured by the ladder scale (Adler et al., 2000; Kraus et al., 2009) and empathic accuracy by the absolute value of differences between rating participants' emotions and estimating a partner's emotions during the hypothetical job interview. As an index of contextual explanations, the degree to which participants focused on context in looking back on their decisions in a resource-allocation task (another task conducted before measuring participants' empathic accuracy) was judged by two independent coders. Considering full mediation of contextual explanations, even if individuals are in high SES environments, an experimental manipulation or activation of contextual explanations might lead them to high empathic accuracy. In future research, an experimental approach based on attributional manipulation (e.g., Weiner & Kukla, 1970; Riemer, 1975) would be useful for examining this possibility.

Examination of the Effectiveness of the Shift-Persist Strategy for Female Undergraduates in Japan (Study 3; Unpublished Data)

Although Study 2 suggests the benefits of low SES (in other words, the pitfalls of high SES), the fact that low SES individuals manage to live in harsh environments is left unaffected or unchangeable. As introduced in the earlier section, low SES undergraduates are sensitive to dissimilarities with other departmental members or to other members' responses to them (Johnson et al., 2011; Kraus et al., 2012), and low SES undergraduates felt concerns about discrimination based on one's social class more strongly than high SES undergraduates (Rheinschmidt & Mendoza-Denton, 2014). Therefore, it is important to find a way to maintain the psychological functioning or mental health of low SES individuals for both basic and applied or clinical researches.

We think that the key is the shift-persist strategy for low SES individuals, as proposed in Chen and Miller (2012). In order to address why low SES is not always bad for health, Chen and Miller (2012) proposed a "shift-and-persist" model to explain the psychobiological mechanisms involved. This model postulates that, if children in the midst of adversity find positive role models who teach them that the world has others that they can depend on and trust, they are more likely to use reappraisals to change how they think about stressful situations that they encounter in the future. Experiencing this positive foundation during childhood then allows some disadvantaged children to develop a "shift and persist" approach (Chen & Miller, 2012, pp. 136-137). Here, shifting is hypothesized to involve cognitive reappraisals (i.e., reframing the meaning of a stressor to be less threatening; seeing the good that can come from difficult life situations) as a form of emotion regulation, and persisting is hypothesized to develop purpose in life and maintain the hope that, despite adversity, the future may be better (Chen, Mclean, & Miller, 2015). To borrow Chen's phrases, this combination of shifting and approaches is adaptive specifically for dealing with adversity. In addition, it reduces physiological responses acutely among low-SES individuals while, in the long-term, mitigating the progression of pathogenic processes leading to chronic diseases.

Consistent with their proposal, experimental evidences demonstrated that the shift-persist strategy was effective for low SES individuals. For example, Chen, Miller, Lachman, Gruenewald, and Seeman (2012) utilized a national sample of U.S. adults and assessed the childhood circumstances from which they came. Their shifting tendency was measured by scales of secondary control coping (positive reappraisals) and emotion regulation (emotional reactivity to stress), and persisting was determined by a measure of future thinking. In addition, Chen et al., (2012) focused on multiple system indices of physiological risk, captured by allostatic load. A composite index of allostatic load was created by biological assessments consisting of 24 different measures across seven physiological systems as a main outcome. In the results of hierarchical multiple regression analyses, there emerged a three-way interaction of childhood SES, shift, and persist variables predicting allostatic load. This interaction showed that shift and persist scores interacted to predict allostatic load among adults from low-SES childhood backgrounds but not among those from high-SES childhood backgrounds. In other words, those who engaged in high shift and high persist strategies in low SES had the lowest allostatic load, whereas this pattern was not found for those in high SES, thus suggesting no benefits of the shift and persist strategies for high SES individuals.

Recently, Chen et al., (2015) focused on another important aspect of biological mechanisms: the role of inflammation. In previous studies, the benefits of shift-and-persist in low-SES individuals were documented for not only physiological risk (Chen et al., 2012) but also clinical outcomes such as obesity and asthma (Kallem et al., 2013; Chen et al., 2011), suggesting no examination of more in-depth inflammatory mechanisms that might underlie shift-and-persist. In order to provide the first test of whether a psychological buffering factor can potentially affect SES disparities in how inflammatory responses occur and are regulated, Chen et al., (2015) developed a new brief measure of shift-and-persist and examined the effect of individuals' shift-and-persist tendencies on inflammatory responses to microbial challenge and increased sensitivity to cortisol signaling. In the experiment, participants comprised 122 adolescents and 122 parents from a diverse range of SES backgrounds. In the results of hierarchical multiple regression analyses, as SES declined, shift-and-persist was associated with greater sensitivity to glucocorticoids' anti-inflammatory properties in both adolescents and adults, and, also, with less low-grade, chronic inflammation. In contrast, as SES increased, the opposite pattern was evident. Taken together, for both adolescents and adults, the shift-and-persist strategies form one type of adaptive psychosocial characteristics and have the potential to regulate inflammatory processes in ways that may mitigate risk for a number of chronic diseases; particularly among disadvantaged groups (Chen et al., 2015).

The series of Chen's research introduced here suggested the benefits of the shift-and-persist strategies for low SES individuals. In Study 3, we attempted to provide the first evidence from a Japanese sample of these benefits. This enables us to demonstrate the reproducibility of Chen's findings and provide an opportunity to expand research on the shift-and-persist strategies in Japan. For this purpose, we conducted a questionnaire survey among Japanese female undergraduates. As the main outcomes, we focused on the participants' self-esteem and depressive tendencies. Given the benefits of the shift-and-persist strategies for low SES individuals (as Chen's findings pointed out), we expected that, for those who are low SES, the high level of shift and persist would be related to their high level of self-esteem or low depressive tendencies. For those of high SES, by contrast, this pattern would not emerge.

Sixty-nine female undergraduates who were enrolled in a junior college in western Japan participated in Study 3 (average age = 18.96 years, SD = 1.78). The questionnaire was described as part of a general survey for several studies in a research project titled "self and group." After this pre-brief for the questionnaire, participants completed the following three scales: the shift-and-persist measure, the trait self-esteem scale, and the depression scale. Participants responded to a Japanese version of the shift-and-persist measure developed by Chen et al., (2015). Reliability and validity of the shift-and-persist measure were demonstrated across both adolescents and adults in their research. The shift-and-persist measure consisted of four items of persisting and shifting and four distractors scored on a five-point scale. Examples of persisting were "I feel my life has a sense of purpose" and "I believe that there is a larger reason or purpose for my life." Examples of shifting were "I think about the positive aspects, or the good that can come from the situation" and "I think about what I can learn from the situation." We translated this measure into Japanese through discussion and asked a professor who had experience of studying abroad to recheck our translation. Regarding participants' self-esteem, we used a Japanese version of Rosenberg's (1965) self-esteem scale (Yamamoto, Matsui, & Yamanari, 1982), which consisted of 10 items scored on a five-point scale. Regarding their depressive tendency, we used the Todai Health Index, as in the first study of Study 1. Five items of each were randomly picked in order to reduce participants' task load. Also, indexes of their subjective SES were reused, because they participated in another experiment and responded to scales that were identical to those in the second study of Study 1.

As described previously, we expected that only for those who are in low SES would the high level of shift and persist be related to the high level of their self-esteem or low depressive tendencies. In order to examine this prediction, we conducted an exploratory factor analysis of the persisting and shifting measure. We subsequently carried out multiple regression analyses regarding three-way interaction of subjective SES, shift, and persist variables predicting participants' self-esteem or depressive tendencies.

First, after finding that a two-factor solution was the best solution based on the MAP (minimum average partial correlation) and a parallel analysis, we performed an exploratory factor analysis with the maximum-likelihood method and promax oblique rotation to assess the structure of the persisting and shifting measure. The results showed the same pattern as Chen's findings: one factor was persisting and the other was shifting. However, one item of a persisting factor ("I feel my life is going nowhere"), which assumed the reverse item, was positively loaded on this factor, similar to the other three items. Thus, we performed the same analysis with seven items, except for this item, because of the match between each conceptual definition of shifting and persisting, and item contents. The results again showed the same pattern as the former version. Table 2 presents the final factor pattern and correlation coefficients among factors and reliabilities.

Table 2. Factor Loadings for Shift-and-Persist Measure

items	Factor1	Factor2	communarity
Shifting			
I think about what I can learn from the situation	**.925**	-.109	.790
I think about what good things could come from the situation	**.616**	.048	.404
I think about what I can learn from the situation	**.575**	.082	.373
I think about the positive aspects, or the good that can come from the situation	**.546**	.047	.320
Persisting			
I believe that there is a larger reason or purpose for my life	-.019	**.847**	.705
My life feels worthwhile	.104	**.751**	.635
I feel my life has a sense of purpose	-.033	**.718**	.499
factorial correlations	**.379**		
α coefficients	**.762**	**.818**	
Mean (SD)	**2.46(0.54)**	**2.62(0.63)**	

Factor 1 was shifting and factor 2 was persisting. In order to stop reducing our sample-size by missing value, we calculated participants' factorial scores of persisting and shifting with the full information maximum likelihood method, using this to examine our prediction. Similarly, we used each factorial score and took the same approach regarding trait self-esteem (Mean = 3.08, SD = 0.84) and depressive tendencies (Mean = 1.86, SD = 0.53). As in Study 2, participants' overall SES scores were created by principal component analysis.

Next, for examination of our prediction, we performed multiple regression analyses of participants' self-esteem scores (the high score represented low train self-esteem). The predictors were participants' factorial scores for persisting and shifting, as well as overall SES, and the three-way interaction effects. Centered persisting and shifting scores and overall SES scores were entered into the equation at Step 1, three types of two-way interaction values were entered at Step 2, and three-way values were entered at Step 3. In the multiple regression analysis, the main effect of overall SES score was significant: $b = -0.37$, $t(57) = -3.02$, $p < .001$. This effect showed that a high level of SES was related to high self-esteem. Importantly, the three-way interaction was significant: $b = 0.31$, $t(56) = -2.36$, $p = .02$, as consistent with our prediction. In analyses of the simple slopes (as depicted in Figures 5 and 6), for participants with low SES (- 1SD) and high shifting (+ 1SD), persisting scores were negatively related to low trait self-esteem, implying high self-esteem by high persisting: $b = -0.78$, $t(56) = -2.49$, $p = .02$. This pattern did not emerge for participants with low SES (- 1SD) and low shifting (- 1SD), $b = -0.14$, $t(56) = -0.50$, $p = .62$, participants with high SES (+ 1SD) and low shifting (- 1SD), $b = -0.29$, $t(56) = -1.33$, $p = .19$, and participants with high SES (+ 1SD) and high shifting (+ 1SD), $b = 0.20$, $t(56) = 0.64$, $p = .53$. These results suggested that those who were in low SES benefited engaging in high shift and high persist strategies. In contrast, this pattern was not found for those in high SES. These results supported Chen's findings of no benefits of the shift and persist strategies for high SES individuals.

As other patterns of simple slope analyses, for participants with high persisting (+ 1SD) and high shifting (+ 1SD), overall SES composite scores were not related to low self-esteem: $b = 0.26$, $t(56) = 1.00$, $p = .32$. Conversely, overall SES composite scores were negatively related to low self-esteem, implying high self-esteem by high SES, in the case of participants with low persisting (- 1SD) and low shifting (- 1SD), $b = -0.56$, $t(56) = -2.76$, $p = .01$, participants with high persisting (+ 1SD) and low shifting (- 1SD), $b = -0.70$, $t(56) = -2.41$, $p = .02$, and participants with low persisting (- 1SD) and high shifting (+ 1SD), $b = -0.64$, $t(56) = -2.32$, $p = .02$. Moreover, for participants with low SES (- 1SD) and high persisting (+ 1SD), their shifting scores were negatively related to low self-esteem, implying high self-esteem by high shifting: $b = -0.75$, $t(56) = -2.34$, $p = .02$. This pattern did not emerge for participants with low SES (- 1SD) and low persisting (- 1SD), $b = -0.09$, $t(56) = -0.32$, $p = .75$, participants with high SES (+ 1SD) and low persisting (- 1SD), $b = -0.18$, $t(56) = -.75$, $p = .46$, and participants with high SES (+ 1SD) and high persisting (+ 1SD), $b = 0.32$, $t(56) = 1.03$, $p = .31$. These results were also consistent with Chen's findings of no benefits of the shift and persist strategies for high SES individuals.

Relatedly, in the case of using SES factorial score with the full information maximum likelihood method, we obtained parallel patterns of SES composite scores (three-way interaction: $b = 0.27$, $t(60) = -2.12$, $p = .04$; persisting for participants with low SES (- 1SD) and high shifting (+ 1SD): $b = -0.72$, $t(60) = -2.45$, $p = .02$). In contrast, multiple regression analyses of participants' depressive tendencies showed a significant main effect of persisting with both SES composite scores ($b = -0.30$, $t(60) = -2.20$, $p = .03$) and SES factorial scores ($b = -0.32$, $t(64) = -2.47$, $p = .02$) only. High persisting scores were negatively related to depressive tendencies.

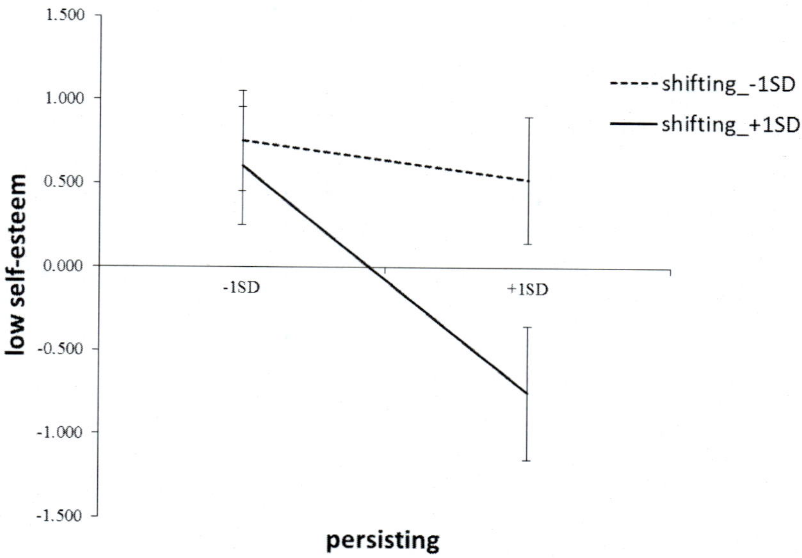

Figure 5. Self-esteem as a function of shifting and persisting for low SES participants (error bars are shown as standard error).

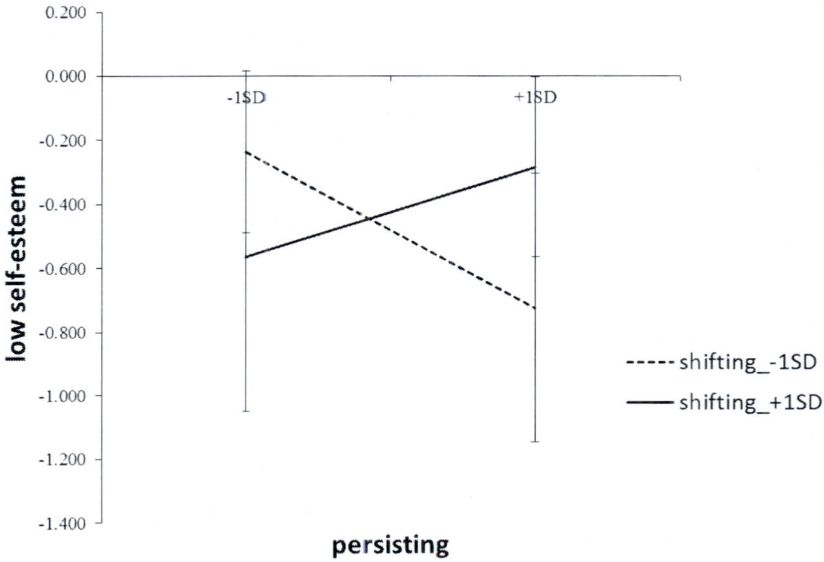

Figure 6. Self-esteem as a function of shifting and persisting for high SES participants (error bars are shown as standard error).

The findings of Study 3 provided us with two important suggestions. First, a Japanese version of the shifting and persisting measure was creditable from the perspective of construct validity. As Chen and Miller (2012) pointed out, this approach of shifting and persisting balances adaptation to stress by shifting oneself while at the same time persisting in life. In other words, it is effective for low SES individuals to deal with varieties of adversity by accepting stress and adjusting oneself to it through emotion regulation strategies such as reappraisals, as well as enduring adversity with strength by finding meaning and maintaining optimism. This combination of approaches is particularly beneficial for low SES individuals in that it reduces their physiological responses acutely, while, in the long-term, it mitigates the progression of pathogenic processes leading to chronic diseases (Chen & Miller, 2012). Related to this point, for participants who were in low SES and engaged in high shifting, their persisting scores were negatively related to low trait self-esteem, implying high self-esteem on the basis of high persisting. The same patterns were obtained for participants who were in low SES and engaged in high persisting. Moreover, for participants who engaged in high persisting and shifting, their overall SES scores were not related to low self-esteem. These findings corresponded with Chen and Miller's model of how shift-and-persist strategies lead to health benefits among low SES individuals. Subsequent research into these strategies was expected to spread in Japan and to contribute to understanding the intrapersonal and interpersonal effects of SES.

Second, focusing on the asymmetry effects of shift-and-persist strategies on psychological functioning and mental health is useful to refine this model. In Study 3, we treated trait-self-esteem as one indicator of psychological functioning and depressive tendency as mental health, along with previous research (e.g., Adler et al., 2000; Chen & Paterson, 2006; Nakashima & Yanagisawa, 2015). Chen and colleagues' research did not fully focus on psychological response, although psychological responses were included in Chen and Miller's model of shift-and-persist strategies. Therefore, our approach was expected to elaborate this model from different views. As introduced in the results of Study 3, although there was a main effect of persisting on participants' depressive tendencies, three-way interaction emerged for their trait-self-esteem. These findings advise against incorporating psychological functioning and mental health in a common tent, though the persisting strategy is more important than shifting in that it affected both psychological functioning and mental health. Further research is needed to resolve the reason why this combination of shifting and persisting strategies is effective for the psychological functioning (not mental health) of low SES individuals, utilizing the experimental and questionnaire approach in a careful manner.

Although Study 3 is valuable in that it provided the initial findings of shifting and persisting strategies using a Japanese sample, we think that additional examination is needed and interesting. In particular, a "jumped-up" effect of shifting and persisting strategies on social rank deserves to be examined. Chen and Miller (2012) emphasized the importance of role models for acquiring these strategies. In their article, the model of shifting and persisting strategies proposed that, in the midst of adversity, some children find role models who teach them to trust others, better regulate their emotions, and focus on their futures. The strategies matured by role models give children a variety of benefits in their later lives. However, their research did not fully consider whether children and adolescents who engaged in these strategies would break through reproduction of SES disparity or poverty as noted in Fujita (2012), which means that, when children in low SES grow up, they are forced to nurture their children in low SES. If shifting and persisting strategies enable children in low SES to ascend in social rank (in other words, to acquire a high level of objective SES such as attaining high academic achievement or finding a good salary and secure job), these strategies seem to be more attractive in creating roots for solving real issues involved in SES. Future research is thus needed to examine whether these strategies would lessen the relationship between childhood SES and present/future SES for low SES individuals in a positive way.

CONCLUSION

In this chapter, we introduced three different studies regarding the benefits and pitfalls of high SES. Study 1 (Nakashima & Yanagisawa, 2015) focused on subjective SES and departmental identity, which interacted to reduce depressive tendencies and negative affective responding. This emphasized the benefits of high SES in that undergraduates with higher subjective SES were likely to gain more benefits from group identity. In contrast, Study 2 and Study 3 emphasized the pitfalls of high SES. Study 2 found that low-SES undergraduates more accurately identified the target's psychological pain and negative feelings in the social exclusion situation than did high-SES participants, which implied negative effects of high SES on interpersonal relationships. Study 3 showed that, for undergraduates who are in low SES, the high level of shift and persist was related to the high level of their self-esteem or low depressive tendencies whereas, for those in high SES, this pattern did not emerge. Moreover, the Japanese version of the shifting and persisting measure was creditable from construct validity.

Nevertheless, these studies are not without their limitations. There is a common limitation through the three studies: a relatively small sample size made up of predominantly female undergraduates. It is important to examine our findings for broader samples, although samples did not arise in an imbalance of participants' gender, and gender difference was less important in relevant research (e.g., Chen & Miller, 2012; Johnson et al., 2011; Kraus et al., 2010; Kraus et al., 2012). This is because many researchers pointed out the importance of reproducibility of psychological science (Buck, 2015; McNutt, 2014). Relatedly, Open Science Collaboration (2015) conducted a large-scale, collaborative effort to obtain an initial estimate of the reproducibility of psychological science, and only 36% of replications had significant results. In other words, over 60% of previous findings failed to be replicated. In order to maintain our findings, future research should ensure broader samples with a balance of participants' gender.

In conclusion, we emphasize the importance of finding ways of masking high and low SES pitfalls or weaknesses. If a researcher finds that low SES is less beneficial than high SES for individuals, he or she may manage to dissolve the disparity of SES. Unfortunately, this attempt seems to be nearly impossible in a capitalist society such as Japan. However, along with *yin and yang* in Chinese culture, by focusing on high and low SES pitfalls or weaknesses we are able to find ways to mask them. Based on the findings of Study 2, even if individuals are in high SES environments, an intervention approach to contextual explanations might lead them to high empathic accuracy. Moreover, shifting and persisting is the very strategy for overcoming the weaknesses of low SES. We hope that many researchers, including us, find a variety of ways of masking high and low SES pitfalls or weaknesses in future research.

References

Aiken, L. S., & West, S. G. (1991). Multiple regression: Testing and interesting interactions. Newbury Park, CA: Sage.

Adler, N. E., Boyce, T., Chesney, M. A., Cohen, S., Folkman, S., Kahn, R. L., & Syme, S. L. (1994). Socioeconomic status and health: The challenge of the gradient. *American psychologist*, 49(1), 15–24.

Adler, N. E., Epel, E. S., Castellazzo, G., & Ickovics, J. R. (2000). Relationship of subjective and objective social status with psychological and physiological functioning: Preliminary data in healthy white women. *Health Psychology*, 19(6), 586–592.

Adler, N. E., Marmot, M., McEwen, B., & Stewart, J. (Eds.). (1999). *Annals of the New York Academy of Sciences: Vol. 896. Socioeconomic status and health in industrial nations: Social, psychological, and biological pathways.* New York: New York Academy of Sciences.

Baumeister, R. F., DeWall, C. N., Ciarocco, N. J., & Twenge, J. M. (2005). Social exclusion impairs self-regulation. *Journal of Personality and Social Psychology*, 88(4), 589–604.

Buck, S. (2015). Solving reproducibility. *Science*, 348(6242), 1403.

Chen, E., Matthews, K. A., & Boyce, W. T. (2002). Socioeconomic differences in children's health: How and why do these relationships change with age? *Psychological Bulletin*, 128(2), 295–329.

Chen, E., McLean, K. C., & Miller, G. E. (2015). Shift-and-persist strategies: associations with socioeconomic status and the regulation of inflammation among adolescents and their parents. *Psychosomatic Medicine*, 77(4), 371–382.

Chen, E., & Miller, G. E. (2012). "Shift-and-persist" strategies: Why low socioeconomic status isn't always bad for health. *Perspectives on Psychological Science*, 7(2), 135–158.

Chen, E., Miller, G. E., Lachman, M. E., Gruenewald, T. L., & Seeman, T. E. (2012). Protective factors for adults from low childhood socioeconomic circumstances: The benefits of shift-and-persist for allostatic load. *Psychosomatic Medicine*, 74(2), 178–186.

Chen, E., & Paterson, L. Q. (2006). Neighborhood, family, and subjective socioeconomic status: How do they relate to adolescent health? *Health Psychology*, 25(6), 704–714.

Chen, E., Strunk, R. C., Trethewey, A., Schreier, H. M., Maharaj, N., & Miller, G. E. (2011). Resilience in low-socioeconomic-status children with asthma: Adaptations to stress. *Journal of Allergy and Clinical Immunology*, 128(5), 970–976.

Côté, S., Kraus, M. W., Cheng, B. H., Oveis, C., Van der Löwe, I., Lian, H., & Keltner, D. (2011). Social power facilitates the effect of prosocial orientation on empathic accuracy. *Journal of Personality and Social Psychology*, 101(2), 217–232.

Côté, S., & Miners, C. T. H. (2006). Emotional intelligence, cognitive intelligence, and job performance. *Administrative Science Quarterly*, 51(1), 1–28.

Dohrenwend, B. P., Levav, I., Shrout, P. E., Schwartz, S., Naveh, G., & Link, B. G. (1992). Socioeconomic status and psychiatric disorders: the causation-selection issue. *Science*, 255(5047), 946–52.

Dubois, D., Rucker, D. D., & Galinsky, A. D. (2015). Social class, power, and selfishness: When and why upper and lower class individuals behave unethically. *Journal of Personality and Social Psychology*, 108(3), 436–449.

Eysenck, H. J., & Eysenck, S. B. G. (1975). *Manual of the Eysenck Personality Questionnaire*. San Diego, CA: EdITS.

Fletcher, G. J. O., & Kerr, P. S. G. (2010). Through the eyes of love: Reality and illusion in intimate relationships. *Psychological Bulletin*, 136(4), 627–658.

Fox, A. J., Goldblatt, P. O., & Jones, D. R. (1985). Social class mortality differentials: Artifact, selection, or life circumstances? *Journal of Epidemiology and Community Health*, 39(1), 1–8.

Frank, R. H. (1999). *Luxury fever: Why money fails to satisfy in an era of excess.* New York, NY: Free Press, Princeton University.

Fujita, H. (2012). Influences of modern poverty on children's development and schooling. *Japanese Journal of Developmental Psychology*, 23(4), 439–449.

Griskevicius, V., Tybur, J. M., Delton, A. W., & Robertson, T. E. (2011). The influence of mortality and socioeconomic status on risk and delayed rewards: A life history theory approach. *Journal of Personality and Social Psychology*, 100(6), 1015-1026.

Haan, M., Kaplan, G., & Syme, S. L. (1989). Socioeconomic status and health: Old observations and new thoughts. In J. Bunker, D. Gomby, & B. Kehrer (Eds.), *Pathways to health: The role of social factors* (pp. 76–135). Menlo Park, CA: Henry J. Kaiser Family Foundation.

Ickes, W., Stinson, L., Bissonnette, V., & Garcia, S. (1990). Naturalistic social cognition: Empathic accuracy in mixed-sex dyads. *Journal of Personality and Social Psychology*, 59(4), 730–742.

Iimura, N., Naragino, H., Ninomiya, K., Matsubayashi, T., Ebina, M., Katada, N., …Fukuchi, M. (2002). Wong - Baker no feisu sukēru no nippon niokeru datō sei to shinrai sei. [The validity and reliability of a Japansese version of the Faces Pain Scale]. *Journal of Japanese Society of Child Health Nursing*, 11(2), 21–27.

Johnson, J. G., Cohen, P., Dohrenwend, B. P., Link, B. G., & Brook, J. S. (1999). A longitudinal investigation of social causation and social selection processes involved in the association between socioeconomic status and psychiatric disorders. *Journal of Abnormal Psychology*, 108(3), 490–499.

Johnson, S. E., Richeson, J. A., & Finkel, E. J. (2011). Middle class and marginal? Socioeconomic status, stigma, and self-regulation at an elite university. *Journal of Personality and Social Psychology*, 100(5), 838–852.

Kallem, S., Carroll-Scott, A., Rosenthal, L., Chen, E., Peters, S. M., McCaslin, C., & Ickovics, J. R. (2013). Shift-and-persist: A protective factor for elevated BMI among low-socioeconomic-status children. *Obesity*, 21(9), 1759–1763.

Karasawa, M. (1991). Toward an assessment of social identity: The structure of group identification and its effects on in-group evaluations. *British Journal of Social Psychology*, 30(4), 293–307.

Kaye, S., Folsom, A., Prineas, R., Potter, J., & Gapstur, S. (1990). The association of body fat distribution with lifestyle and reproductive factors in a population study of post-menopausal women. *International Journal of Obesity*, 14(7), 583–591.

Knowles, M. L., & Gardner, W. L. (2008). Benefits of membership: The activation and amplification of group identities in response to social rejection. *Personality and Social Psychology Bulletin*, 34(9), 1200–1213.

Kraus, M. W., Côté, S., & Keltner, D. (2010). Social class, contextualism, and empathic accuracy. *Psychological Science*, 21(11), 1716–1723.

Kraus, M. W., & Keltner, D. (2009). Signs of socioeconomic status: A thin-slicing approach. *Psychological Science*, 20(1), 99–106.

Kraus, M. W., & Park, J. W. (2014). The undervalued self: social class and self-evaluation. *Frontiers in Psychology*, 5, 1404.

Kraus, M. W., Piff, P. K., & Keltner, D. (2009). Social class, the sense of control, and social explanation. *Journal of Personality and Social Psychology*, 97(6), 992–1004.

Kraus, M. W., Piff, P. K., & Keltner, D. (2011). Social class as culture: The convergence of resources and rank in the social realm. *Current Directions in Psychological Science*, 20(4), 246–250.

Kraus, M. W., Piff, P. K., Mendoza-Denton, R., Rheinschmidt, M. L., & Keltner, D. (2012). Social class, solipsism, and contextualism: How the rich are different from the poor. *Psychological Review*, 119(3), 546–572.

Lachman, M. E., & Weaver, S. L. (1998). The sense of control as a moderator of social class differences in health and well-being. *Journal of Personality and Social Psychology*, 74(3), 763–773.

McNutt, M. (2014). Reproducibility. *Science*, 343(6168), 229.

Murayama, K. (2012). *Datousei: Gainen no rekishi teki hensen to shinrisokuteigaku teki kanten kara no kosatu*. [Validity: Historical and psychometric perspectives]. *Kyoiku shinri gaku kenkyū*, 51, 118–130. (In Japanese with English abstract.).

Nakashima, K. (2014). Hihaisekisha eno kyōkan niyoru shinritekiitami no densen nitsuite no jikkentekikentōi [Experimental study of infection with social pain by empathizing with excluded individuals]. *Hattatsu kenkyū*, 28, 117–129. (In Japanese with English abstract.).

Nakashima, K., Isobe, C., & Ura, M. (2012). Ingroup representation and social value affect the use of ingroup identification for maintaining and enhancing self-evaluation. *Asian Journal of Social Psychology*, 15(1), 49–59.

Nakashima, K., Isobe, C., & Ura, M. (2013). How does higher in-group social value lead to positive mental health? An integrated model of in-group identification and support. *Asian Journal of Social Psychology*, 16(4), 271–278.

Nakashima, K, & Yanagisawa, K. (2015). Subjective socioeconomic status and departmental identity interact to reduce depressive tendencies and negative affective responding for female undergraduates. *Japanese Psychological Research*, 57(2), 113–125.

Nesdale, D., & Lambert, A. (2007). Effects of experimentally manipulated peer rejection on children's negative affect, self-esteem, and maladaptive social behavior. *International Journal of Behavioral Development*, 31(2), 115–122.

Nikolaev, B., & Rusakov, P. (2015). Education and happiness: an alternative hypothesis. *Applied Economics Letters*, 1–4.

Oakes, J. M., & Rossi, P. H. (2003). The measurement of SES in health research: Current practices and steps toward a new approach. *Social Science and Medicine*, 56(4), 769–784.

Open Science Collaboration. (2015). Estimating the reproducibility of psychological science. *Science*, 349(6251), aac4716.

Oreopoulos, P., & K. G. Salvanes. 2011. "Priceless: The Nonpecuniary Benefits of Schooling." *The Journal of Economic Perspectives*, 25(1), 159–184.

Piff, P. K., Kraus, M. W., Côté, S., Cheng, B. H., & Keltner, D. (2010). Having less, giving more: The influence of social class on prosociality. *Journal of Personality and Social Psychology*, 99(5), 771–784.

Rheinschmidt, M. L., & Mendoza-Denton, R. (2014). Social class and academic achievement in college: The interplay of rejection sensitivity and entity beliefs. *Journal of Personality and Social Psychology*, 107(1), 101–121.

Riemer, B. S. (1975). Influence of causal beliefs on affect and expectancy. *Journal of Personality and Social Psychology*, 31(6), 1163–1167.

Rosenberg, M. (1965). *Society and the adolescent self-image*. Princeton, NJ: Princeton University Press.

Singh-Manoux, A., Marmot, M. G., & Adler, N. E. (2005). Does subjective social status predict health and change in health status better than objective status? *Psychosomatic Medicine*, 67(6), 855–861.

Smart Richman, L., & Leary, M. R. (2009). Reactions to discrimination, stigmatization, ostracism, and other forms of interpersonal rejection: A multimotive model. *Psychological Review*, 116(2), 365–383.

Solís, C. B., Kelly-Irving, M., Fantin, R., Darnaudéry, M., Torrisani, J., Lang, T., & Delpierre, C. (2015). Adverse childhood experiences and physiological wear-and-tear in midlife: Findings from the 1958 British birth cohort. *Proceedings of the National Academy of Sciences*, 112(7), 738–746.

Stinson, L., & Ickes, W. (1992). Empathic accuracy in the interactions of male friends versus male strangers. *Journal of Personality and Social Psychology*, 62(5), 787–797.

Suzuki, S., Aoki, S., Kawa, M., Yanai, H., Saito, Y., & Hosoki, T. (1979). Identification of neurotics and schizophrenics from the respective reference normal group by a paper health questionnaire, the Todai Health Index. *Japanese Journal of Behaviormetrics*, 6, 28–38. (In Japanese with English abstract.).

Takata, T. (2000). On the scale for measuring independent and interdependent view of self. *Bulletin of Research Institute of Nara University*. 8, 145–163 (In Japanese).

Weiner, B., & Kukla, A. (1970). An attributional analysis of achievement motivation. *Journal of Personality and Social Psychology*, 15(1), 1–20.

Williams, K. D. (2007). Ostracism. *Annual Review of Psychology*, 58(1), 425–452.

Williams, K. D. (2009). Ostracism: A temporal need-threat model. In M. P. Zanna (Ed.), *Advances in Experimental Social Psychology* (Vol. 41, pp. 275–314). New York: Academic Press.

Yamamoto, M., Matsui, Y. & Yamanari, Y. (1982). Recognized components of various sides of self. *Japanese Journal of Educational Psychology*, 30, 64–68.

Yanagisawa, K. (2011). *The effects of psychosocial resources on adaptation after social exclusion*. Unpublished doctoral dissertation, Hiroshima University, Hiroshima.

Yanagisawa, K., Masui, K., Furutani, K., Nomura, M., Yoshida, H., & Ura, M. (2013). Family socioeconomic status modulates the coping-related neural response of offspring. *Social Cognitive and Affective Neuroscience*, 8(6), 617–622.

Zaki, J., & Ochsner, K. (2009). The need for a cognitive neuroscience of naturalistic social cognition. *Annals of the New York Academy of Sciences*, 1167, 16–30.

Zaki, J., & Ochsner, K. N. (2012). The neuroscience of empathy: Progress, pitfalls and promise. *Nature Neuroscience*, 15(5), 675–680.

BIOGRAPHICAL SKETCH

Name: Ken'ichiro Nakashima

Affiliation: Department of Psychology, Graduate School of Education, Hiroshima University

Education: Hiroshima University (Graduate school of Integrated Arts and Sciences), Ph. D. (philosophy), 2010

Address: 1-1-1, Kagamiyama, Higashi-Hiroshima City, 739-8524 JAPAN

Research and Professional Experience:

Lecturer, Preschool Education Section in Nagasaki Women's Junior College (from April 1, 2010 to September 30, 2013).

Lecturer, Department of Psychology, Graduate School of Education, Hiroshima University (from October 1, 2013 to March 31, 2016)

Associate professor, Department of Psychology, Graduate School of Education, Hiroshima University (from April 1, 2016 to present)

Honors:

A Grant-in-Aid for Research Activity Start-up (number 22830128) from the Japan Society for the Promotion of Science (2010-2011)

Hattatu Kagaku Kenkyu Kyoiku Syoreisyo from Center of Developmental Education and Research in Japan (2012)

A Grant-in-Aid for Young Scientists (B) (number 25780399) from the Japan Society for the Promotion of Science (2013-2015)

The grant funding from the Mazda Foundation in Japan (2015-2017)

Publication Last 3 years

1. Nakashima, K., Yanagisawa, K., & Ura, M. (2013). Dissimilar effects of task-relevant and interpersonal threat on independent-interdependent self-construal in individuals with high self-esteem. *Asian Journal of Social Psychology*, 16(1), 50–59.
2. Nakashima, K., Kawamoto, T., Isobe, C., & Ura, M. (2013). Differential Responses of Independent and Interdependent People to Social Exclusion. *International Journal of Psychological Studies*, 5(1), 31–44.

3. Nakashima, K. (2013). Infection with social pain by empathizing with excluded individuals. *Human Developmental Research*, 27, 189–194.
4. Nakashima, K., Isobe, C., Souma, T., & Ura, M. (2013). Asymmetric effect of in-group social values on identity with common-identity and common-bond in-groups. *The Japanese Journal of psychology*, 84(2), 162–168.
5. Nakashima, K., Isobe, C., & Ura, M. (2013). How does higher in-group social value lead to positive mental health? An integrated model of in-group identification and support. *Asian Journal of Social Psychology*, 16(4), 271–278.
6. Nakashima, K. (2014). Chapter14 Who uses in group identification and favoritism for buffering threats to self-esteem, and when do they use it? In J. H. Borders (Ed.), *Handbook on the Psychology of Self-Esteem* (pp. 251–276), New York: NOVA Science Publishers.
7. Nakashima, K., & Yanagisawa, K. (2015). Subjective socioeconomic status and departmental identity interact to reduce depressive tendencies and negative affective responding for female undergraduates. *Japanese Psychological Research*, 57(2), 113–125.
8. Shimizu, H., Nakashima, K., & Morinaga, Y. (in press). Role of Defensive Pessimism in Interpersonal Communication by Focusing on Behavioral Intention with Others. *The Japanese Journal of Personality*, 24(3), 202–214.
9. Furukawa, Y., Nakashima, K., & Morinaga, Y. (2016). Influence of social context on the relationship between guilt and prosocial behaviour. *Asian Journal of Social Psychology*, 19(1), 49–54.
10. Nakazato, N., Nakashima, K., & Morinaga, Y. (in press). The importance of freedom in the East and the West over time: A meta-analytic study of predictors of well-being. *Social Indicators Research*.
11. Furukawa, Y., Nakashima, K., & Morinaga, Y. (in press). Effect of induced guilt on compensatory behavior toward the victim in a resource allocation among three people paradigm in Japan. *Japanese Journal of Social Psychology*.

In: Socioeconomic Status
Editor: Geoffrey Perkins

ISBN: 978-1-63485-326-2

Chapter 6

WHO SEEKS RELATIONSHIPS WITH DARK TRIAD INDIVIDUALS AND HOW? FOCUSING ON SOCIOECONOMIC STATUS AND TRAIT SELF-CONTROL

Yuri Tasaki[1,*], Ken'ichiro Nakashima[1] and Mitsuhiro Ura[2]

[1]Hiroshima University, Graduate School of Education, Hiroshima, Japan
[2]Otemon Gakuin University, Faculty of Psychology, Osaka, Japan

ABSTRACT

Who seeks relationships with Dark Triad individuals and how? To answer these questions, this chapter reports the findings of two questionnaire surveys focusing on the effects of socioeconomic status and trait self-control on seeking these relationships. The socially undesirable behaviors (Spain et al., 2014) and attitudes (Jones, 2013) of the Dark Triad have recently drawn attention in the field of social and personality psychology. According to Paulhus and Williams (2002), the Dark Triad is defined as a constellation of three socially undesirable personality traits that include the tendency to seek admiration and special treatment

---

* Corresponding author: Yuki Tasaki, Hiroshima University, Graduate School of Education, 1-1, Kagamiyama 1-chome, Higashi-Hiroshima, 739-8524, Japan. E-mail: kasou0129@gmail.com. This research was supported by a Grant-in-Aid (number 15H03449) from the Japan Society for the Promotion of Science.

(narcissism), to be callous and insensitive (psychopathy), and to engage in interpersonal manipulation (Machiavellianism). Previous studies have focused mainly on the negative aspects of Dark Triad traits, pointing out that individuals high in Dark Triad traits are antisocial and inhumane. However, some individuals are socially successful, acquiring prestigious jobs such as politicians and lawyers even if they have psychopathy tendencies within the Dark Triad (Mullins-Sweatt et al., 2010). Therefore, there is a possibility that the Dark Triad traits are not necessary maladaptive. The reasons for this are still unknown.

The authors propose that a particular type of individual may seek relationships with Dark Triad individuals; that is, low socioeconomic status individuals. There is a possibility that the Dark Triad individuals would be comfortable in these interpersonal relationships because low socioeconomic status individuals are prone to connect with them and may acquire successful lifestyles in some cases. In addition, low trait self-control would mediate the relationship between low trait self-control and seeking relationships with Dark Triad traits. In order to examine these possibilities, the authors conducted two questionnaire surveys using a hypothetical scenario in which participants either faced the most critical situation in their lives (Study 1) or a non-crisis situation (Study 2) and a Dark Triad character offered them help.

In Study 1 (N = 671), we obtained two main findings. First, low socioeconomic status led individuals to low trait self-control, which, in turn, contributed to seeking help from individuals with high Dark Triad traits more often when in crisis. Second, the tendency of individuals with low socioeconomic status to seek those with Dark Triad traits was pronounced in interpersonally-related stressful events (the loneliness or irritation experiences). However, we could not judge whether low SES individuals have a similar pattern in non-crisis situations because Study 1 focused on the most critical situation in their lives. Moreover, based on the similarity-attraction hypothesis (e.g., Byrne & Nelson, 1965; Byrne, 1969), in addition to the mediating effects of trait self-control, it is important to examine whether individuals with high Dark Triad traits would be willing to seek relationships with Dark Triad others, considering their trait self-control. In order to examine this point carefully, we conducted an online survey focused on help in non-crisis situations in Study 2 (N = 663). Results showed two findings. First, mediating effects of trait self-control between SES and seeking help from others with high Dark Triad traits did not emerge in non-crisis situations. Second, participants with high Dark Triad traits sought others with high Dark Triad traits in non-crisis scenarios, regardless of their trait self-control. In contrast, participants with low trait self-control and low Dark Triad traits sought others with high Dark Triad traits. Considering the findings of our two studies, the importance of self-control training or intervention was discussed in future directions for research on socioeconomic status and Dark Triad traits.

INTRODUCTION

The Dark Triad comprises three distinct but overlapping constructs: psychopathy, Machiavellianism, and narcissism (Furnham, Richards, & Paulhus, 2013; Lee & Ashton, 2005; Paulhus & Williams, 2002). Here, psychopathy is characterized by enduring antisocial behavior, impulsivity, selfishness, callousness, and remorselessness (Skeem, Polaschek, Patrick, & Lilienfeld, 2011; Wai & Tiliopoulos, 2012). Machiavellianism comprises a selfish, manipulative propensity motivated by instrumentality (Jakobwitz & Egan, 2006; Jones & Paulhus, 2010). Narcissism is characterized by behavioral grandiosity, pride, egotism, and a lack of empathy (Kohut, 1977; Pincus & Lukowitski, 2010). Although each of these three constructs has some unique features not shared by the other two, they appear to share some common elements such as exploitation, manipulativeness, and a grandiose sense of self-importance (Lee & Ashton, 2005). In other research, moreover, the Dark Triad personality presents over time (Foster, Campbell, & Twenge, 2003) and across various world regions (Schmitt, 2008), suggesting the universal and trans-cultural nature of the Dark Triad. This construct is involved in negative personal and social outcomes such as limited empathy and has thus been considered undesirable (e.g., Bushman & Baumeister, 1998; Hare, 1996; Jonason, Lyons, Bethell, & Ross, 2013).

Considering the core elements of the Dark Triad personality such as low empathy, callousness, and manipulative propensity, individuals seem to avoid interpersonal relationships with others who have a high Dark Triad personality. In relationships with others who have a manipulative propensity within Dark Triad traits, individuals may be used as tools and may thus be exhausted. Alternatively, in relationships with others who are callous, it may be difficult for individuals to receive social support (which is beneficial for individuals) and to expect others to understand their mind. Because individuals are able to estimate these potential negative outcomes easily, it is natural that, if they can, individuals will not seek interpersonal relationships with others who are of high Dark Triad personality.

In fact, recent research provided us with the findings supporting the folk wisdom mentioned above. Lyons, Marcinkowska, Helle, and McGrath (2015) investigated female preference for computer-manipulated Dark Triad male faces in two online studies. The results indicated that women rated the high psychopathy and narcissistic faces the most masculine; moreover, women showed a low preference for the high morphs in both long and short-term relationships. Lyons et al., (2015) suggested that this low preference could be based on the idea that potential costs such as risking injury or desertion outweigh any putative benefits such as genes for offspring when women pair up with high Dark Triad men. In a similar vein, Lyons and Simeonov (2016) confirmed the same pattern whereby women had weak preference for high Dark Triad faces across short and long-term mating contexts, using a different sample from that of Lyons et al., (2015). Considering that the Dark Triad traits are associated with sexual aggression (Bushman, Bonacci, Van Dijk, & Baumeister, 2003; Jones & Olderbak, 2014; Kosson, Kelly, & White, 1997), which could be detrimental for marital relations, the abovementioned profit-and-loss arithmetic for mating is plausible.

Given that women's preference regarding men expands to general interpersonal relationships (e.g., friendship and intragroup relations), individuals with Dark Triad traits seem to be prone to loneliness, resulting in them being selected from others less frequently. Relatedly, previous research has reported negative intrapersonal and interpersonal outcomes in terms of social loneliness. Berkman and Syme (1979) showed that people who lacked social and community ties were more likely to die in the follow-up period than those with more extensive contacts, using the 1965 Human Population Laboratory survey of a random sample of 6928 adults in Alameda County. Moreover, the age-adjusted relative risks for those most isolated when compared to those with the most social contacts were 2.3 for men and 2.8 for women. Adopting a similar approach, Eng, Rimm, Fitzmaurice, and Kawachi (2002) sampled 28,369 US male health professionals aged 42–77 years in 1988. They showed that, over 10 years, the relative risk of total mortality for men in the lower two levels of social integration compared with more socially-integrated men was 1.19 after controlling for age, occupation, health behaviors, and so on. Other research that focused on the 15 school shootings between 1995 and 2001 found that these shootings were precipitated by social rejection or loneliness. In other words, acute or chronic rejection—in the form of ostracism, bullying, and/or romantic rejection—was present in all but two of the incidents (Leary, Kowalski, Smith, & Phillips, 2003). Considering these findings, individuals with the Dark Triad personality may carry potential risk based on social rejection or loneliness, resulting in maladjustment or a socially unsuccessful life.

Nevertheless, other research provided us with findings that go against folk wisdom or other relevant findings. One typical example of contrary evidence is successful psychopaths (Hall & Benning, 2006; Mullins-Sweatt, Glover, Derefinko, Miller, & Widiger, 2010). Successful psychopaths are individuals who fit the criteria of a psychopath in theory, having certain fundamental traits such as callousness, but largely succeed in their exploitation (Mullins-Sweatt et al., 2010). In other research (Ishikawa, Raine, Lencz, Bihrle, & Lacasse, 2001), they were defined as community-based psychopaths who escape conviction for their crimes. These research studies are common in suggesting that there are socially successful individuals who nevertheless have high psychopathy tendencies and are driven to the unsuccessful or non-socially applicable behavior of committing crime. Although there has been little empirical research characterizing such persons, Mullins-Sweatt et al., (2010) sampled psychologists with an interest in law, along with attorneys and clinical psychology professors, to obtain descriptions of individuals considered to be psychopaths who were also successful in their endeavors. This study showed a consistent description across professions and a convergence with descriptions of traditional psychopathy. These findings suggest that the existence of successful psychopathy should be considered in light of the difference whereby the successful psychopathy profile had higher scores on conscientiousness than did unsuccessful psychopathy. Given that socially successful states imply good interpersonal relationships for individuals with high psychopathy tendencies, it is natural that individuals with Dark Triad traits (including psychopathy) may have a way to connect with others.

Previous research suggested that individuals with a Dark Triad personality might have good (but not perfect) interpersonal skills or tactics, such as a protean approach to interpersonal influence. Jonason and Webster (2012) found that the Dark Triad traits correlate with a number of unique tactics of influence. In other words, each trait provides for a variety of tactics of interpersonal influence, creating a veritable toolbox of means to manipulate others. If individuals seek out patterns in an environment as a means of predicting events, having multiple tactics may reduce predictability and therefore enable an individual to avoid detection. Although the protean approach has its limits (this choice of tactic seems insensitive to the relationship with the target it seeks to manipulate), it might be useful for individuals high in these traits to modulate their choice of tactics of influence. In other research, Bereczkei (2015) focused on the cognitive devices and their neural correlates underlying Machiavellian decision making. He pointed out that Machiavellians can efficiently exploit others, which is likely to arise from their flexible problem-solving processes in changing environmental circumstances, although they appear to have a relatively poor mindreading ability and emotional intelligence. He also proposed that Machiavellians have specialized cognitive domains of decision making, which entail monitoring others' behavior, task orientation, and so on. Consistent with these suggestions, in recent research focused on the influence of the Dark Triad and communication condition (face-to-face versus computer-mediated communication) on success in negotiations, Crossley, Woodworth, Black, and Hare (2016) found that individuals scoring higher on the Dark Triad performed best when they negotiated face-to-face with their counterparts based on overall success in the negotiation.

In this chapter, we approach the interpersonal relationships of Dark Triad traits from a different view to that of previous research, raising the possibility that others seek relationships with Dark Triad individuals. On this point, Lyons and Simeonov (2016) provided us with suggestive findings. As noted above, they found that Dark Triad facial morphs were aversive, irrespective of the mating context and environmental scarcity for women. Importantly, Machiavellian faces were disliked significantly less in the resource wealthy than in the resource scarce condition, and especially as short-term mating partners. Lyons and Simeonov (2016) suggested that any putative fitness costs associated with mating with Machiavellian men (e.g., the potential for aggression and desertion) were slightly reduced when the environment was wealthy. The possibility that others seek relationships with Dark Triad individuals in a certain condition is thus left unaddressed. Based on this logic, we focused on socioeconomic status as another relevant factor.

Socioeconomic status (SES) is defined as material wealth, occupation, and participation in educational and social institutions (Oakes & Rossi, 2003). Thus, SES can be measured objectively in terms of family income and educational attainment; that is, so-called objective SES (Lachman & Weaver, 1998). Individuals *do* possess a subjective sense of SES based on these objective indicators, such as family income and educational attainment (Kraus, Piff, Mendoza-Denton, Rheinschmidt, & Keltner, 2012). Multiple studies have also suggested a link between SES and the sense of control. For example, Lachman and Weaver (1998) examined the differences of SES in two aspects of the sense of control (mastery and perceived constraints) in three national probability samples. They found that participants with lower income (which was one objective indicator of SES) had lower perceived mastery and higher perceived constraints than participants with higher income. Kraus, Piff, and Keltner (2009) also showed that social rank (which was one subjective indicator of SES) determined a lowered sense of control. In addition, subjective SES led individuals to a lower sense of control, which, in turn, contributed to lower self-regulation in a Japanese sample (Takebe & Matsuzaki, 2015).

In other research, this tendency of low SES individuals was found to be amplified by threat situation or manipulation. For example, mortality cues shifted individuals from lower SES childhoods toward a faster strategy prioritizing mating effort and early reproduction over heavy somatic investment. Conversely, for individuals who grew up in higher SES environments, mortality cues motivated them to want to delay reproduction, consistent with shifting to a slower strategy (Griskevicius, Tybur, Delton, & Robertson, 2011). In this research, the authors pointed out that a faster strategy is associated with preference for more risk whereas a slower strategy is associated with preference for less risk, resulting in low SES (particularly childhood SES) individuals managing to live in risk. This suggestion corresponded with other findings indicating that exposure to uncertainty led individuals from poorer childhoods to have a significantly lower sense of control than those from wealthier childhoods, which, in turn, determined their impulsive behaviors (Mittal & Griskevicius, 2014). Considering the link between self-regulation and impulsive and compulsive decision-making (Faber & Vohs, 2011) in addition to these findings, individuals with low SES are thought to accept offers from individuals with Dark Triad traits who may constitute a potential risk for them. This is because individuals with low SES are prone to engage in less deliberate decision making or short-term thinking. That is, there is a possibility that individuals with low SES seek relationships with Dark Triad individuals. We set this as a main prediction in this chapter and examined it through two online surveys. We introduced the first study in detail as follows.

Study 1

In order to provide initial evidences for this possibility, we conducted a questionnaire survey using a hypothetical scenario in which each participant faced the most critical situation in his/her life. After reading this scenario, participants were asked to accept help from those who have Dark Triad characteristics. In other words, where their supporters had Dark Triad traits, participants judged whether they would seek to engage in an interpersonal relationship with these supporters. If our prediction is correct, participants with lower SES would accept offers from supporters who possess Dark Triad traits more readily than participants with higher SES because of low self-control on the part of individuals with lower SES.

Given that self-control plays an important role in the process whereby individuals with low SES seek relationships with Dark Triad individuals, their tendencies would be amplified by other situational factors that add further pressure to their self-control. From this perspective, we focused on interpersonal stressful events such as social loneliness and daily hassle. In previous research, social exclusion impaired self-regulation or self-control resources such that participants who were led to anticipate a lonely future were less able to make themselves consume a healthy but bad-tasting beverage, and these participants quit sooner on a frustrating task (Baumeister, Dewall, Ciarocco, & Twenge, 2005). Relevant studies also found that social exclusion (which may cause social loneliness) led to maladaptive behaviors such as aggression or impulsivity (Leary, Kowalski, Smith, & Phillips, 2003) and cognitive-emotional avoidance resulting in reduced self-awareness (Twenge, Catanese, & Baumeister, 2003). Furthermore, irritating situations led participants to less self-regulated states of impaired persistence on a subsequent task (Wallace & Baumeister, 2002). Based on these findings, interpersonal stressful events such as social loneliness and daily hassle seem to worsen self-control for individuals with low SES. As a result, there is a possibility that the process through which individuals with low SES seek relationships with Dark Triad individuals would be pronounced in socially lonely or daily hassle situations. In other words, we predicted seeking behaviors for individuals with the Dark Triad traits as a function of SES and loneliness (or daily hassle).

METHODS

Participants and Procedure

Six hundred and seventy-one volunteers (28% male, 72% female; mean age 21.12 years) participated in an online survey via Rakuten Research in exchange for payment.

Our survey consisted of two sections. The first survey at Time 1 occurred in November 2014 (T1). The second survey at Time 2 occurred in January 2015 (T2). In order to investigate the prediction that lower SES individuals would seek support from those with Dark Triad traits as a result of low self-control, we used participants' SES, self-control, and the degree of seeking relationships with Dark Triad individuals at T1. Next, in order to investigate the prediction that tendencies of individuals with low SES would be pronounced in socially lonely or daily hassle situations, we used participants' SES, loneliness or daily hassle, and the degree of seeking relationships with Dark Triad individuals at T2. In addition, we focused on the change of their seeking tendencies from T1 to T2.

During the T1 testing session, we first asked participants to take part in a survey on personality. Participants were assessed using the following two measures: the Japanese version of the Dark Triad Dirty Dozen (DTDD) scale (Tamura, Oshio, Tanaka, Masui, & Jonason, 2015) and the Japanese version of the Trait Self-Control (SC) scale (Mishima, 2008). The DTDD scale was translated from Jonason and Webster's (2010) original scale and comprised three subscales: 'Psychopathy,' 'Machiavellianism,' and 'Narcissism.' Examples were, "I tend to want others to admire me," "I tend to lack remorse," and "I have used deceit or lied to get my way." Participants responded to 12 items, using a 5-point Likert scale ranging from 1 (strongly agree) to 5 (strongly disagree). The items were averaged to create scores ($\alpha = .86$). The SC scale was translated from Tangney, Baumeister, and Boone's (2004) original scale. Examples were, "I am good at resisting temptation" and "I never allow myself to lose control." Participants responded to 36 items, using a 5-point Likert scale ranging from 1 (strongly agree) to 5 (strongly disagree). The items were averaged to create scores ($\alpha = .86$).

Participants were then asked to read a scenario in which the most critical situation in their life was assumed. The details were as follows: you are in the biggest mess of your life. You must fight against the enemy and win in order get out of a hole. Then, a supporter appears. The individual never lets you down because he/she feels an obligation to you. In addition, the individual has social power and therefore benefits you. After reading this scenario, we asked participants the degree to which they would seek support from those who have the Dark Triad traits, utilizing the Dark Triad Dirty Dozen of Other (DTDD-O) scale. In particular, following the question of "do you accept the offer if the individual has the tendencies as follows?" we presented participants with a modified version of the Dark Triad Dirty Dozen (Tamura et al., 2015). Examples of the scale items were "The individual tends to lack remorse" and "The individual tends to want others to admire them." The DTDD-O scale was a 12-item scale, using a 5-point Likert scale ranging from 1 (strongly agree) to 5 (strongly disagree). Finally, participants were asked their annual household income of last year as an indicator of SES.

At T2, 254 of the 671 volunteers returned and completed questionnaires on the same scale as those of T1 except for two measures: the Japanese version of the revised UCLA Loneliness scale (Moroi, 1992) and daily hassles scale (Munakata, Nakao, Fujita, & Suwa, 1986). The revised UCLA Loneliness scale was assessed with items such as, "I lack companionship" and "There is no one I can turn to." Participants responded to 20 items, using a 5-point Likert scale ranging from 1 (strongly agree) to 4 (strongly disagree). The items were averaged to create scores for subscales ($\alpha = .94$). The daily hassles scale was assessed with items such as, "How many hassles do you feel about own future?" and "How many hassles do you feel about own health?" Participants responded to 30 items, using a 3-point Likert scale ranging from 1 (strongly agree) to 3 (strongly disagree). The items were averaged to create scores for subscale ($\alpha = .93$).

RESULTS

Preliminary Data Analyses

Regarding the DTDD-O scale made up of 12 items, after finding that a two-factor solution was the best solution based on the MAP (minimum average partial correlation) and a parallel analysis, we first performed an exploratory factor analysis using the maximum-likelihood method and promax oblique rotation to assess the structure of this scale. However, one item was equally loaded on each factor. We again performed the same analysis with 11 items, except for this item (Table 1). One factor represented items connected with psychopathy and Machiavellianism. The other factor represented items connected with narcissism. We therefore averaged scores on relevant items to create scores for subscales (psychopathy and Machiavellianism $\alpha = .89$; narcissism $\alpha = .90$).

Examination of Mediating Effects of Self-Control (Prediction 1)

To examine prediction 1, we conducted mediation analysis. The analysis was conducted via bootstrap analysis using Preacher and Hayes's (2004) guidelines. From the result of the analysis (with 2,000 samples), it was found that lower SES individuals sought support from a hypothetical supporter with psychopathy and Machiavellianism due to low self-control. It showed a significant direct effect of SES on psychopathy and Machiavellianism: β = -.07, SE = .04, p = .08. The effect of SES on psychopathy and Machiavellianism was reduced to non-significance, β = -.02, SE = .04, p = .66, when controlling for the mediator of SC, which still had a significant impact: β = -.27, SE = .04, p = 0.00; 95% bias-corrected CI [-.09, -.03]. The 95% bias-corrected confidence interval for the size of the indirect effect excluded zero, suggesting a significant indirect effect (MacKinnon, Fairchild, & Fritz, 2007). Similarly, results of the analysis (with 2,000 samples) tended to indicate a significant direct effect of SES on narcissism: β = -.07, SE = .04, p = .07. The effect of SES on narcissism was reduced to non-significance, β = -.03, SE = .04, p = .48, when controlling for the mediator of SC, which still had a significant impact: β = -.22, SE = .04, p = .01; 95% bias-corrected CI [-.08, -.02]. In sum, a significant indirect effect was confirmed in the case of narcissism, similar to psychopathy and Machiavellianism.

Table 1. Factor pattern of the Dark Triad Dirty Dozen of Other (DTDD-O) scale Component

Item	Factor1	Factor2
psychopathy and Machiavellianism		
4. Individual who tends to exploit others towards my own end.	**.844**	-.090
8. Individual who tends to be cynical.	**.774**	-.064
5. Individual who tends to lack remorse	**.701**	.037
2. Individual has used deceit or lied to get his/her way.	**.642**	.121
11. Individual who tends to seek prestige or status.	**.624**	.119
1. Individual who tends to manipulate others to get his/her way.	**.614**	.127
10. Individual who tends to want others to pay attention to his/her.	**.613**	.231
narcissism		
6. Individual who tends to not be too concerned with morality or the morality of his/her actions.	-.048	**.915**
9. Individual who tends to want others to admire oneself.	.015	**.851**
3. Individual has use flattery to get his/her way.	-.005	**.814**
12. Individual who tends to expect special favors from others.	.222	**.616**

Seeking Behaviors for Individuals with the Dark Triad Traits as a Function of SES and Interpersonal Stressful Events (Prediction 2)

Next, we used the data at T1 and T2 in order to examine to our second prediction. Namely, that interpersonal stressful events such as social loneliness and daily hassle would worsen self-control for individuals with low SES. As a result, the process whereby individuals with low SES seek relationships with Dark Triad individuals would be pronounced in socially lonely or daily hassle situations.

To examine this prediction, we first generated scores for the change in participants' narcissism scores or the psychopathy and Machiavellianism score of the DTDD-O scale using the following method. A simple regression analysis was used to generate participants' residual scores, which represented the degree of seeking relationships with others who had a tendency for with narcissism or psychopathy and Machiavellianism at Time 2, controlling for seeking tendencies at Time 1. High levels of each residual score therefore indicated an increase in the degree of seeking relationships with these individuals.

Second, we performed multiple regression analyses of narcissism residual scores or the psychopathy and Machiavellianism residual score of the DTDD-O scale. The predictors were participants' household annual income and loneliness. We regressed the DTDD score as a control variable in Step 0, adding the centered income and loneliness score in Step 1. The two-way interaction values were entered into the equation at Step 2. The hierarchical regression results are shown in Table 2. In the results, the two-way interaction of narcissism was not significant (β = -.06, t (249) = -.93, ns.), but psychopathy and Machiavellianism were marginally significant (β = -.12, t (249) = -1.93, $p < .10$). In analyses of the simple slopes as suggested by Aiken and West (1991) and depicted in Figure 1, the loneliness scores of participants with low income (- 1SD) were positively related to psychopathy and Machiavellianism residual scores: β = .15, t (249) = 1.78, $p < .10$. This pattern did not emerge for participants with high income (+ 1SD): β = −.08, t(249) = −.80, ns.

Table 2. Hierarchical Regression Models Predicting loneliness at low SES conduse to seek relationships with psychopathy and Machiavellianism individuals

	Predictor	β	t-value	R^2-change	F-value
Step0					
	Dark Triad	0.19	2.99 **	0.04	9.62
Step1					
	SES	0.04	0.65	0.00	0.38
	loneliness	0.04	0.55		
Step2					
	SES × loneliness	-0.12	-1.93 +	0.01	3.71
model		*R^2=0.05, F(4, 249)=3.54***			

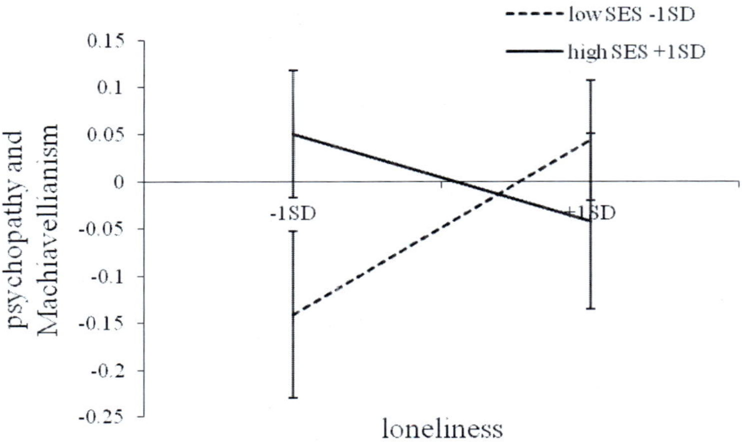

Figure 1. Psychopathy and Machiavellianism residual scores as SES and loneliness (error bars are shown as standard error).

Table 3. Hierarchical Regression Models Predicting Daily hassles at low SES conduse to seek relationships with psychopathy and Machiavellianism individuals

	Predictor	β	t-value	R^2-change	F-value
Step0					
	DTDD	0.16	2.56 *	0.04	9.62
Step1					
	SES	0.03	0.41	0.01	1.33
	Daily hassles	0.09	1.35		
Step2					
	SES × Daily hassles	-0.11	-1.79 +	0.01	3.19
model		R^2=0.06, F(4, 249)=3.90*			

$^{**}p < .01$, $^{*}p < .05$, $^{+}p < .10$

Next, to examine the impact of daily hassle, we conducted the same approach in relation to social loneliness. The predictors were participants' household annual income and the daily hassles score. We regressed the DTDD score as a control variable in Step 0, adding the centered income and daily hassles score in Step 1. The two-way interaction values were entered into the equation at Step 2. The hierarchical regression results are shown in Table 3. In the results of the multiple regression analysis, the two-way interaction of narcissism was not significant (β = -.05, t (249) = -.71, ns.), but psychopathy and Machiavellianism were marginally significant (β = -.11, t (249) = -1.79, p < .10). In analyses of the simple slopes, as depicted in Figure 2, the daily hassles scores for participants with low income (- 1SD) were positively related to psychopathy and Machiavellianism residual scores: $\beta = .35$, $t(249) = 2.37$, $p < .10$. This pattern did not emerge for participants with high SES (+ 1SD): $\beta = -.02$, $t(249) = -.24$, ns.

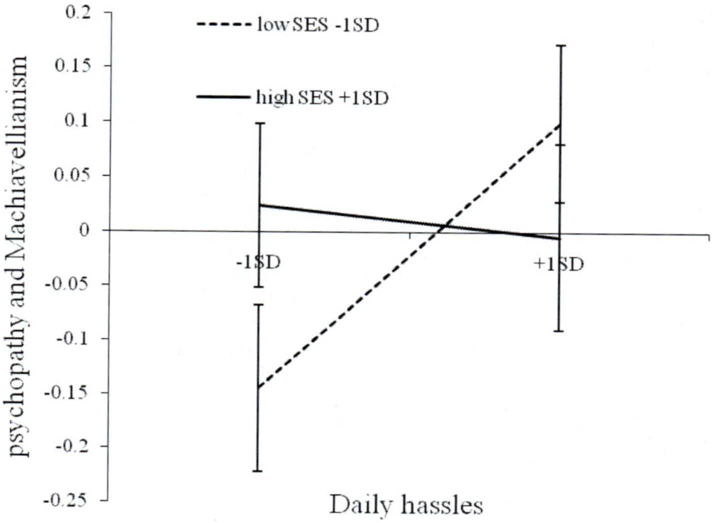

Figure 2. Residual of psychopathy and Machiavellianism scores as SES and daily hassles (error bars are shown as standard error).

DISCUSSION

The findings of Study 1 provided us with two important suggestions. First, participants with lower SES were more likely to accept offers from supporters with Dark Triad traits than were participants with higher SES, the reason being the low self-control of individuals with lower SES. Considering the findings of several research studies (e.g., Faber & Vohs, 2011; Mittal & Griskevicius, 2014; Takebe & Matsuzaki, 2015), individuals with low SES are thought to accept offers from individuals with Dark Triad traits because individuals with low SES opt to engage in less deliberate decisions or short-term thinking. In other words, they would engage in impulsive behavior derived from their low self-control, resulting in them seeking relationships with Dark Triad individuals who may be a potential risk for themselves. Second, seeking relationships with Dark Triad individuals on the part of individuals with low

SES was pronounced in socially lonely or daily hassle situations. Considering that interpersonal stressful events worsen self-control (Baumeister et al., 2005; Leary et al., 2003), the findings of Study 1 suggested that socially lonely or daily hassle situations led individuals with low SES to self-regulation resource depletion, resulting in their amplified tendency to seek relationships with Dark Triad individuals.

Nonetheless, Study 1 is limited in a number of ways. First, although Study 1 provided important suggestions regarding seeking help from individuals with high Dark Triad traits, we could not judge whether low SES individuals have a similar pattern in non-crisis situations. This is because Study 1 focused on the most critical situations in an individual's life only. Second, analyses of Study 1 controlled for participants' Dark Triad tendencies per se, and, therefore, Study 1 did not discuss roles of individuals' Dark Triad tendencies in this seeking process. Based on the similarity-attraction hypothesis (e.g., Byrne & Nelson, 1965; Byrne, 1969), it is plausible that individuals with high Dark Triad traits are willing to seek relationships with Dark Triad others. Therefore, we also need to examine this point from the perspective of the similarity-attraction hypothesis.

Study 2

Based on these reasons, we conducted a questionnaire survey using a hypothetical scenario in which participants faced the non-critical situation in their lives. Participants were asked to accept help from those who possessed some individual characteristics of the Dark Triad traits, as in Study 1. Where their supporters had these Dark Triad traits, participants judged whether they would seek to be in an interpersonal relationship with such supporters as their general or basic pattern (i.e., not a situation-specific pattern).

We have two predictions for seeking relationships with Dark Triad others. First, individuals would prefer others who share similar personality traits would thus build interpersonal relationships with similar others. This similarity-attraction effect regarding attitudes and personality was celebrated as an important finding several decades ago (e.g., Byrne & Nelson, 1965; Byrne, 1969). In light of these findings, we predicted that participants who were high on the Dark Triad scale would more readily accept help from others with individual characteristics entailing Dark Triad traits than would participants who were low on the Dark Triad scale. Second, based on the idea that low self-control could play an important role in determining whether low

SES individuals seek interpersonal relationships with Dark Triad individuals, we predicted that low self-control would lead to being in interpersonal relationships with Dark Triad others; no matter whether the Dark Triad tendencies of participants were high or low.

METHODS

Participants and Procedure

Six hundred and sixty-three volunteers (53% male, 47% female; mean age 40.34 years) participated in an online survey via Rakuten Research in exchange for payment. The survey occurred during November 2014. The procedure and scales were identical to the T1 version of Study 1 except for situations intended to measure participants' general or basic tendencies for seeking others with Dark Triad traits. Here, we asked participants to respond to the Dark Triad Dirty Dozen of Other (DTDD-O) scale without a hypothetical situation. In particular, after asking "if the individuals have tendencies as follows, how much do you accept their offers for help?" we presented participants with the DTDD-O scale and asked them to respond to it.

RESULTS

Self-Control Mediated Between Low SES People and Those High in Dark Triad Traits in a Non-Crisis Situation (Prediction 1)

Before examining prediction 1, we conducted confirmatory factor analysis using DTDD-O based on the pattern of Study 1. Although the model fit indices were not good, $\chi^2(44, N = 663) = 719.89$ $p > .56$, RMSEA = .15, CFI = .83, we averaged scores on relevant items to create scores for subscales given that the alpha reliability was adequately high (psychopathy and Machiavellianism: $\alpha = .88$; narcissism: $\alpha = .87$). Subsequently, we conducted mediation analysis, as in Study 1. However, in the case of psychopathy and Machiavellianism, as well as narcissism, direct effects of SES were not significant (psychopathy and Machiavellianism: $\beta = -.01$, SE = .04, $p = .71$; narcissism: $\beta = -.02$, SE = 0.04, $p = .64$). These findings suggest that the mediating effects of SC were not replicated in a non-crisis condition (in other words, there was no mediation regarding the tendency of seeking others with Dark Triad traits as general or basis patterns).

Individuals Who Are High in Dark Triad Traits Seek Relationships with Dark Triad Others (Prediction 2)

Next, we examined the second prediction: participants who score high on the Dark Triad scale would be more likely to seek relationships with Dark Triad individuals than would participants who score low on the Dark Triad scale. Moreover, low self-control participants would seek relationships with Dark Triad others, regardless of participants' Dark Triad tendencies. First, to examine of our prediction, we performed multiple regression analyses of narcissism scores or psychopathy and Machiavellianism scores (the high score represented accepting offers from others with narcissism or with psychopathy and Machiavellianism, but these were not residual scores because Study 2 was a cross-sectional survey). The predictors were participants' Dark Triad traits and SC, along with the two-way interaction effects. We added centered the Dark Triad traits and the SC scores in Step 1. The two-way interaction values were entered into the equation at Step 2. The hierarchical regression results are shown in Table 4. In the results of the multiple regression analysis, the two-way interaction of narcissism was not significant ($\beta = .07$, t (659) = 1.62, ns.), but that of psychopathy and Machiavellianism was significant ($\beta = .08$, t (659) = 2.05, $p < .05$). In analyses of the simple slopes, as depicted in Figure 3, the SC scores of participants with low Dark Triad traits (- 1SD) were positively related to psychopathy and Machiavellianism scores of DTDD-O, $\beta = -.09$, t (659) = -2.29, $p < .05$. This pattern did not emerge for participants with high Dark Triad traits (+ 1SD), $\beta = .09$, t (659) = .86, ns.

Table 4. Hierarchical Regression Models Predicting SC at DTDD conduse to seek relationships with psychopathy and Machiavellianism individuals

	Predictor	β	t-value	R^2-change	F-value
Step1					
	DTDD	0.46	10.52 **	0.22	77.68
	SC	-0.02	-0.38		
Step2					
	DTDD × SC	0.08	2.06 *	0.01	4.22
model	R^2=0.22, F(3, 659)=3.66**				

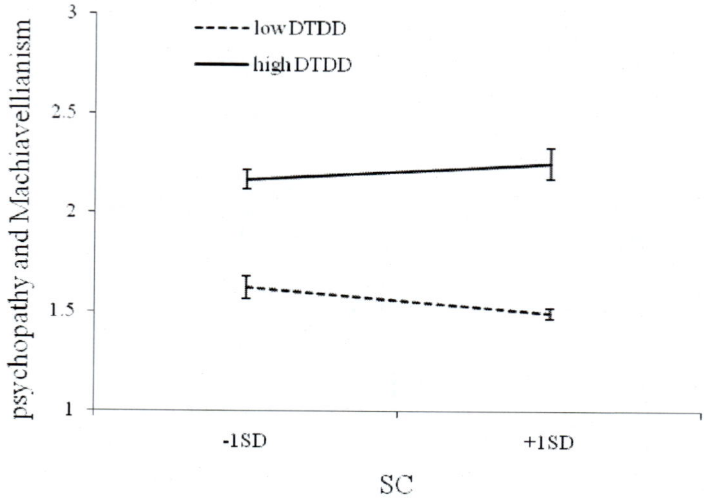

Figure 3. Psychopathy and Machiavellianism scores as DTDD and SC (error bars are shown as standard error).

DISCUSSION

We investigated two further points in Study 2. The first point was whether participants with lower SES would be more likely to accept offers from others who have the Dark Triad traits than would participants with higher SES in a non-crisis situation (as general or basis patterns for participants with lower SES). We thought that this process would emerge because of low self-control for individuals with lower SES. The second was whether participants who were high on the Dark Triad scale would be more likely to seek relationships with Dark Triad others than would participants who were low on the Dark Triad scale. The results of mediation analyses suggested that self-control did not mediate the relationship between SES and seeking relationships with others who had Dark Triad traits. This pattern did not support our first prediction. In contrast, we found that participants with low trait self-control and low Dark Triad traits accepted offers from others with high Dark Triad traits, and participants with high Dark Triad traits did so regardless of their self-control. These results partially supported our second prediction and suggested that self-control played an important role for individuals with low Dark Triad traits (not but individuals with low SES, as shown in Study 1).

Further research should examine the effects of interpersonal-situational factors such as social loneliness and daily hassle in seeking others with Dark Triad traits, as in Study 1. Considering the lack of mediating effects of self-control in non-crisis situations, the amplifying effects of social loneliness and daily hassle as shown in Study 1 should be retested. This would enable us to clarify the boundary condition of these amplifying effects, leading to an understanding of interpersonal relationships with Dark Triad individuals. If self-control played an important role in seeking others with Dark Triad traits, as we consistently proposed in this chapter, the amplifying effects of social loneliness and daily hassle would emerge for individuals with low self-control and low Dark Triad traits (as opposed to individuals with high Dark Triad traits). This is because self-control did not influence this seeking pattern for individuals with high Dark Triad traits. This prediction should be examined in future research.

GENERAL DISCUSSION

In this chapter, we conducted two online surveys in order to reveal who seeks relationships with Dark Triad individuals and how, focusing on socioeconomic status and trait self-control. In Study 1, we used the hypothetical scenario of crisis. When those with Dark Triad traits appeared as supporters in this situation, participants indicated willingness to receive their support. We obtained two main findings. First, low SES led individuals to low trait self-control, which, in turn, contributed to high acceptance of support from those with Dark Triad traits. In other words, individuals who are in low SES seek relationships with Dark Triad individuals because of low self-control. This process derives from individuals with low SES being prone to engage in less deliberate decisions or short-term thinking. This idea also corresponds with relevant findings regarding the link between subjective SES and a sense of control (Kraus et al., 2009; Takebe & Matsuzaki, 2015), and the link between self-regulation and impulsive and compulsive decision making (Faber & Vohs, 2011).

Second, in the results of hierarchical multiple regressions, these tendencies of low SES were amplified by interpersonal-situational factors that add further pressure to their self-control: social loneliness and daily hassle. Low SES individuals accepted support from those with Dark Triad traits (in particular, psychopathy and Machiavellianism) as their social loneliness or daily hassle increased. In other words, low SES individuals more strongly seek relationships with Dark Triad individuals in situations of high social loneliness or daily hassle. Considering that social exclusion (which may cause social loneliness) led to maladaptive behaviors (Leary et al., 2003) and irritating situations led participants to less self-regulated states of impaired persistence on a subsequent task (Wallace & Baumeister, 2002), these processes of low SES individuals are plausible. Relatedly, it is important that residual scores of low SES individuals are under zero in the low case of social loneliness or daily hassle, as shown in Figures 1 and 2. This is because these scores suggest that low SES individuals are prone to denying support from those who are high in psychopathy and Machiavellianism if they are in good relationships or non-irritating situations. As stated in the Introduction, Lyons and Simeonov (2016) suggested that any putative fitness costs associated with mating with Machiavellian men (e.g., potential for aggression and desertion) are slightly reduced when the environment is wealthy. Although our perspective differs from that of Lyons and Simeonov (2016), we share the view that situational factors provide a key for answering the question of who seeks relationships with Dark Triad individuals and how.

Although Study 1 provided important findings regarding seeking help from individuals with high Dark Triad traits, we could not judge whether low SES individuals have a similar pattern in non-crisis situations, as Study 1 focused on the most critical situation in an individual's life. In addition, analyses of Study 1 controlled for participants' Dark Triad tendencies per se, and, therefore, Study 1 did not discuss the roles of individuals' Dark Triad tendencies in this seeking process. Based on the similarity-attraction hypothesis (e.g., Byrne & Nelson, 1965; Byrne, 1969), it is plausible that individuals with high Dark Triad traits are willing to seek relationships with Dark Triad others. It is thus important to reveal whether individuals' Dark Triad tendencies and trait self-control interact to predict seeking relationships with Dark Triad others. For this purpose, Study 2 conducted an online survey focused on help in non-crisis situations. Results of mediation analyses suggested that self-control did not mediate the relationship between SES and seeking relationships with others who had Dark Triad traits. In addition, results of hierarchical multiple regressions showed that participants with low trait self-control and low Dark Triad traits accepted offers from others with high Dark Triad traits. In contrast, high Dark Triad participants sought others with high Dark Triad traits, regardless of their self-control.

The two studies introduced in this chapter seem to provide less systematic evidence regarding the question of who seeks relationships with Dark Triad individuals and how. Study 1 revealed the mediating effects of trait self-control whereas Study 2 did not confirm this. Similarly, Study 1 only showed that individuals' SES and situational interpersonally-related factors interacted to predict seeking for individuals with high Dark Triad traits. Moreover, Study 2 revealed individuals' Dark Triad tendencies and trait self-control interacted to predict seeking behaviors. These differences between Study 1 and 2 may derive from differences of crisis. In other words, our two studies seem to propose a comprehensive or broader model of seeking help from individuals with high Dark Triad traits. Nevertheless, considering that this model is based on *significant-trend* results (in particular, the findings of Study 1), we need to retest our findings using different samples or an alternative approach. This is useful from the perspective of reproducibility of psychological science (Buck, 2015; McNutt, 2014).

However, our findings are common in proposing the importance of self-control in this model. As noted above, in Study 1, low SES led individuals to low trait self-control, which, in turn, contributed to high accepting of support from those with Dark Triad traits. In Study 2, low Dark Triad participants with low trait self-control more strongly sought others with high Dark Triad traits. These findings suggest that self-control is an important key for this seeking behavior. In other words, opportunities that impair individuals' self-control or self-regulation such as interpersonally-related events seem to trigger interpersonal tendencies of individuals with low self-control, which involves relationships with Dark Triad individuals. In this regard, previous research demonstrated that cognitive and behavioral training improved individuals' self-control. Denson, Capper, Oaten, Friese, and Schofield (2011) tested whether self-control training over a 2-week period could decrease anger and aggression in response to provocation, and self-control training reduced aggression among those high in trait aggression. In this research, they required participants to use their non-dominant hand between 8:00 a.m. and 6:00 p.m. every day after giving participants some examples (e.g., brushing their teeth, opening doors, drinking with a glass or mug and stirring, and so on). Moreover, Kutsuzawa and Ozaki (2015) demonstrated the effectiveness of other training methods from multiple indicators of self-control. For example, over the course of a 13-day experimental period, participants used a handgrip as long as they could twice a day (handgrip condition), stopped to use their smartphone without something to do (smart phone condition), or were willing to ready themselves for a scenario 5 minutes before the deadline, such as arriving at a meeting room 5 minutes before the starting time (in Japanese, *gohunmae kodo* condition). Future research is needed to examine the effectiveness of these self-control trainings, focusing on seeking behaviors of individuals with low SES (in an interpersonal-difficulty situation: Study 1) or individuals with low Dark Triad traits and low self-control (Study 2).

Finally, we discuss future directions regarding examinations of interpersonal relationships for individuals with high Dark Triad traits. We believe that these approaches offer the path to a greater understanding of Dark Triad traits. First, future research is needed to demonstrate the effects of interpersonal threats on the selection of potential partners with different traits in experimental settings in order to refine the findings of Study 1. The methods and materials of Lyons and Simeonov (2016), in addition to the cyberball paradigm, are useful for this examination. The cyberball paradigm is a computer-based ball-tossing game in which participants interact with two computer-controlled confederates (Williams, Cheung, & Choi, 2000). If the findings of Study 1 are replicated in this setting, it is predicted that low SES participants prefer to partner with Dark Triad facial morphs in the exclusion condition compared to the acceptance condition. Moreover, there is a possibility that this interaction is mediated by participants' temporally impaired self-control. We also think that such an experimental examination may be useful for answering the question of why low SES individuals seek relationships with others who do not possess narcissism but exhibit psychopathy and Machiavellian personalities. Turning to participants' Dark Triad tendencies, another possibility is that individuals with high Dark Triad traits would prefer to partner with Dark Triad facial morphs, regardless of exclusion or acceptance conditions, whereas individuals with low Dark Triad traits would do so in the social exclusion condition. Examinations for these possibilities help us to more clearly answer the research question in this chapter: who seeks relationships with Dark Triad individuals and how?

Second, future research should examine how individuals with Dark Triad traits form interpersonal relationships per se. Beyond relationships with a particular partner, on which Studies 1 and 2 focused, we need to apply another approach regarding the pattern of interpersonal relationships that individuals with Dark Triad traits exhibit. This is because this approach enables us to understand the dynamics of their interpersonal relationships or their strategies. In other words, it would contribute to understanding "Dark Triad people as social animals." As one approach, snowball sampling seems to be useful. This is a sampling method wherein a researcher asks primary participants to respond to a questionnaire and consequently invite secondary participants to respond to a questionnaire. A researcher thus examines what type of secondary participants share relationships with the primary participants. In other words, a researcher could uncover (a part of) the interpersonal relationships of the primary participants. For example, Ishiguro (2010) examined the effects of urbanism on kin and friendship networks in a Japanese context using snowball sampling. This approach enables us to reveal the patterns of interpersonal relationships that individuals with Dark Triad traits develop. Given that participants in low SES (in particular, in social loneliness or daily hassle situations) or participants with low self-control and Dark Triad traits seek relationships with Dark Triad others, as found in Studies 1 and 2, individuals experiencing economical or interpersonal troubles seem to surround Dark Triad individuals. In this interpersonal situation, Dark Triad individuals may rise through the ranks to find social and economic success. We hope that many researchers, including us, contribute to understanding Dark Triad people as social animals in future research.

REFERENCES

Baumeister, R. F., DeWall, C. N., Ciarocco, N. J., & Twenge, J. M. (2005). Social exclusion impairs self-regulation. *Journal of Personality and Social Psychology*, 88(4), 589–604.

Bereczkei, T. (2015). The manipulative skill: Cognitive devices and their neural correlates underlying Machiavellian's decision making. *Brain and Cognition*, 99, 24–31.

Berkman, L. F., & Syme, S. L. (1979). Social networks, host resistance, and mortality: a nine-year follow-up study of Alameda County residents. *American Journal of Epidemiology*, 109(2), 186–204.

Buck, S. (2015). Solving reproducibility. *Science*, 348(6242), 1403.

Bushman, B. J., & Baumeister, R. F. (1998). Threatened egotism, narcissism, self-esteem, and direct and displaced aggression: Does self-love or self-hate lead to violence? *Journal of Personality and Social Psychology*, 75(1), 219–229.

Bushman, B. J., Bonacci, A. M., Van Dijk, M., & Baumeister, R. F. (2003). Narcissism, sexual refusal, and aggression: Testing a narcissistic reactance model of sexual coercion. *Journal of Personality and Social Psychology*, 84(5), 1027–1040.

Byrne, D. (1961). Interpersonal attraction and attitude similarity. *The Journal of Abnormal and Social Psychology*, 62(3), 713-715.

Byrne, D. (1969). Attitudes and attraction. In L. Berkowitz (Ed.), *Advances in Experimental Social Psychology* (Vol. 4, pp. 35–89). New York: Academic Press.

Byrne, D., & Nelson, D. (1965). Attraction as a linear function of proportion of positive reinforcements. *Journal of personality and social psychology, 1*(6), 659.

Crossley, L., Woodworth, M., Black, P. J., & Hare, R. (2016). The dark side of negotiation: Examining the outcomes of face-to-face and computer-mediated negotiations among dark personalities. *Personality and Individual Differences*, 91, 47–51.

Denson, T. F., Capper, M. M., Oaten, M., Friese, M., & Schofield, T. P. (2011). Self-control training decreases aggression in response to provocation in aggressive individuals. *Journal of Research in Personality*, 45(2), 252–256.

Eng, P. M., Rimm, E. B., Fitzmaurice, G., & Kawachi, I. (2002). Social ties and change in social ties in relation to subsequent total and cause-specific mortality and coronary heart disease incidence in men. *American Journal of Epidemiology*, 155(8), 700–709.

Faber, R. J., & Vohs, K. D. (2011). Self-regulation and spending: Evidence from impulsive and compulsive buying. In K. D. Vohs & R. F. Baumeister (Eds.), *Handbook of Self-Regulation: Research, Theory, and Applications* (2nd ed., pp. 537–550). New York: Guilford Press.

Foster, J. D., Campbell, W. K., & Twenge, J. M. (2003). Individual differences in narcissism: Inflated self-views across the lifespan and around the world. *Journal of Research in Personality*, 37(6), 469–486.

Furnham, A., Richards, S., & Paulhus, D. (2013). The Dark Triad of personality: A 10 year review. *Social and Personality Compass*, 7(3), 199–216.

Griskevicius, V., Tybur, J. M., Delton, A. W., & Robertson, T. E. (2011). The influence of mortality and socioeconomic status on risk and delayed rewards: a life history theory approach. *Journal of Personality and Social Psychology*, 100(6), 1015–1026.

Hall, J. R., & Benning, S. D. (2006). The ''Successful" psychopath: Adaptive and subclinical manifestations of psychopathy in the general population. In C. J. Patrick (Ed.), *Handbook of Psychopathy* (pp. 459–478). New York: Guilford.

Hare, R. D. (1996). Psychopathy: A clinical construct whose time has come. *Criminal Justice and Behavior*, 23(1), 25–54.

Ishiguro, I. (2010). The effect of urbanism on kin and friendship network in Japanese context. *Studies in the humanities: social sciences*. 23, 29–48.

Ishikawa, S. S., Raine, A., Lencz, T., Bihrle, S., & Lacasse, L. (2001). Autonomic stress reactivity and executive functions in successful and unsuccessful criminal psychopaths from the community. *Journal of Abnormal Psychology*, 110(3), 423–432.

Jakobwitz, S., & Egan, V. (2006). The dark triad and normal personality traits. *Personality and Individual Differences*, 40(2), 331-339.

Jonason, P. K., Lyons, M., Bethell, E. J., & Ross, R. (2013). Different routes to limited empathy in the sexes: Examining the links between the dark triad and empathy. *Personality and Individual Differences*, 54(5), 572–576.

Jonason, P. K., & Webster, G. D. (2010). The Dirty Dozen: A concise measure of the dark triad. *Psychological Assessment,* 22(2), 420-432.

Jonason, P. K., & Webster, G. D. (2012). A protean approach to social influence: Dark Triad personalities and social influence tactics. *Personality and Individual Differences*, 52(4), 521–526.

Jones, D. N. (2013). What's mine is mine and what's yours is mine: The Dark Triad and gambling with your neighbor's money. *Journal of Research in Personality*, *47*(5), 563-571.

Jones, D. N., & Olderbak, S. G. (2014). The associations among dark personalities and sexual tactics across different scenarios. *Journal of Interpersonal Violence*, 29(6), 1050–1070.

Jones, D. N., & Paulhus, D. L. (2010). Different provocations trigger aggression in narcissists and psychopaths. *Social Psychological and Personality Science*, 1(1), 12–18.

Kohut. H. (1977). *The restoration of the self.* New York: International Universities Press.

Kosson, D. S., Kelly, J. C., & White, J. W. (1997). Psychopathy-related traits predict self-reported sexual aggression among college men. *Journal of Interpersonal Violence*, 12(2), 241–254.

Kraus, M. W., Piff, P. K., & Keltner, D. (2009). Social class, sense of control, and social explanation. *Journal of Personality and Social Psychology*, 97(6), 992–1004.

Kraus, M. W., Piff, P. K., Mendoza-Denton, R., Rheinschmidt, M. L., & Keltner, D. (2012). Social class, solipsism, and contextualism: How the rich are different from the poor. *Psychological Review*, 119(3), 546–572.

Kutsuzawa, G., & Ozaki, Y. (2015, September). Development and verification of benefits of self-control training method. Poster session presented at the annual meeting of the Japanese Psychological Association, Nagoya.

Lachman, M. E., & Weaver, S. L. (1998). The sense of control as a moderator of social class differences in health and well-being. *Journal of Personality and Social Psychology*, 74(3), 763–773.

Leary, M. R., Kowalski, R. M., Smith, L., & Phillips, S. (2003). Teasing, rejection, and violence: Case studies of the school shootings. *Aggressive Behavior*, 29, 202–214.

Lee, K., & Ashton, M. C. (2005). Psychopathy, Machiavellianism, and narcissism in the Five-Factor Model and the HEXACO model of personality structure. *Personality and Individual Differences*, 38, 1571-1582.

Lyons, M. T., Marcinkowska, U. M., Helle, S., & McGrath, L. (2015). Mirror, mirror, on the wall, who is the most masculine of them all? The Dark Triad, masculinity, and women's mate choice. *Personality and Individual Differences*, 74, 153–158.

Lyons, M., & Simeonov, L. (2016). The undesirable Dark Triad? Women dislike Dark Triad male faces across different mating context and socio-ecological conditions. *Personality and Individual Differences*, 90, 338–341.

MacKinnon, D. P., Fairchild, A. J., & Fritz, M. S. (2007) Mediation Analysis. *Annual Review of Psychology*, 58, 593-614.

McNutt, M. (2014). Reproducibility. *Science*, 343(6168), 229.

Mishima, S. (2008). Self-regulation process in interpersonal relations: Focus attention on trait self-control. Hiroshima University, Master's thesis.

Mittal, C., & Griskevicius, V. (2014). Sense of control under uncertainty depends on people's childhood environment: A life history theory approach. *Journal of Personality and Social Psychology*, 107(4), 621–637.

Moroi, K. (1992). Dimensions of the revised UCLA Loneliness Scale. *Studies in Humanities*, 42, 23-51.

Mullins-Sweatt, S. N., Glover, N. G., Derefinko, K. J., Miller, J. D., & Widiger, T. A. (2010). The search for the successful psychopath. *Journal of Research in Personality*, 44(4), 554–558.

Munakata, T., Nakao, T., Fujita, K., & Suwa, S. (1986) Stress and mental health degree of urban residents. *Journal of Mental Health*, 32, 49-68.

Oakes, J. M., & Rossi, P. H. (2003). The measurement of SES in health research: Current practices and steps toward a new approach. *Social Science and Medicine*, 56(4), 769–784.

Paulhus, D. L., & Williams, K. M. (2002). The Dark Triad of personality: Narcissism, Machiavellianism, and psychopathy. *Journal of Research in Personality*, 36(6), 556–563.

Pincus, A. L., & Lukowitsky, M. R. (2010). Pathological narcissism and narcissistic personality disorder. *Annual Review of Clinical Psychology*, 6, 421–446.

Preacher, K. J., & Hayes, A. F. (2004). SPSS and SAS procedures for estimating indirect effects in simple mediation models. *Behavior research methods, instruments, & computers*, *36*(4), 717-731.

Schmitt, D. P. (2008). The "Dark Triad" of personality across 58 nations: The evolution of sex differences and cultural variations in anti-sociality. Talk presented at the Human Behavior and Evolution Society meeting in Kyoto, Japan.

Skeem, J. L., Polaschek, D. L., Patrick, C. J., & Lilienfeld, S. O. (2011). Psychopathic personality bridging the gap between scientific evidence and public policy. *Psychological Science in the Public Interest*, 12, 95-162.

Spain, S. M., Harms, P., & LeBreton, J. M. (2014). The dark side of personality at work. *Journal of Organizational Behavior, 35*(S1), S41-S60.

Takebe, M., & Matsuzaki, K. (2015, October) The relationship of subjective socioeconomic status with control feeling and self-regulation: By use of self-regulation scale. Poster session presented at the annual meeting of the Japanese Society of Social Psychology, Tokyo.

Tamura, A., Oshio, A., Tanaka, K., Masui, K., & Jonason, P. K. (2015). Development, reliability, and validity of the Japanese version of Dark Triad Dirty Dozen (DTDD-J). *The Japanese Journal of Personality*, 24, 26-37.

Tangney, J. P., Baumeister, R. F., & Boone, A. L. (2004). High self-control predicts good adjustment, less pathology, better grades, and interpersonal success. *Journal of Personality,* 72(2), 271-322.

Twenge, J. M., Catanese, K. R., & Baumeister, R. F. (2003). Social exclusion and the deconstructed state: Time perception, meaninglessness, lethargy, lack of emotion, and self-awareness. *Journal of Personality and Social Psychology*, 85(3), 409–423.

Wai, M., & Tiliopoulos, N. (2012). The affective and cognitive empathic nature of the dark triad of personality. *Personality and Individual Differences*, 52(7), 794–799.

Wallace, H. M., & Baumeister, R. F. (2002). The effects of success versus failure feedback on further self-control. *Self and Identity*, 1(1), 35–41.

Williams, K. D., Cheung, C. K. T., & Choi, W. (2000). CyberOstracism: Effects of being ignored over the Internet. *Journal of Personality and Social Psychology*, 79(5), 748–762.

RELATED NOVA PUBLICATIONS

SOCIOECONOMIC STATUS AND HEALTH IMPLICATIONS

Sarah Reibert and Alice Jannings

ISBN: 978-1-62100-675-6 Publication Date: 2012

The relation between socioeconomic status and population health is evident in epidemiological studies. Socioeconomic status is typically measured using income and financial resources, occupation type, and educational attainment. In this book, the authors present topical research in the study of socioeconomic status and its health implications. Topics discussed include diabetes, marginality, and gender identity; the socioeconomic aspects of health services in Israel; low socioeconomic status and child mental health disparities; adolescent health risk behavior from a migrant population in the United Arab Emirates; Japanese women's health related to job stress and the hidden costs incurred by families and friends of patients with low health literacy.

Early Childhood Obesity, Socioeconomic Status, and Executive Functioning in Atlanta Children*

Amanda K Brzozowski†, PhD, MPH and Carolyn D Drews-Botsch, PhD, MPH

Emory University, Rollins School of Public Health, Department of Epidemiology, Atlanta, Georgia, US

Prior research has demonstrated negative associations between childhood obesity and executive functioning (EF) in older children. We used data from the Follow-Up Development and Growth Experiences Study (1997-99) to assess the relationship between early childhood obesity (body mass index (BMI), triceps- and subscapular-skinfold-thickness (TST, SST)) and EF (Developmental NEuroPSYchology Assessment (NEPSY), mean = 10, SD = 3). Obesity metrics and NEPSY scores were obtained on 423 children aged 54 months born at one of two Atlanta hospitals – a private hospital with a primarily white, middle class population, and a public hospital with a largely African-American, lower socioeconomic status (SES) population. Covariate information was obtained during the study or from previously collected data. Linear regression was used to estimate the change in NEPSY score associated with being in the top 15th percentile of BMI/TST/SST based on CDC norms. Declines in NEPSY statue score were associated with high TST/SST in girls and high BMI/TST/SST in children born at the private hospital. After stratification by both gender and hospital of birth, the negative association between obesity and NEPSY statue score persisted among girls born at the private hospital. No associations were observed between overweight/obesity and NEPSY visual attention scores, regardless of gender or hospital of birth. While no consistent association was observed between early childhood obesity and EF, among girls born at the private hospital, obesity was associated with declines in NEPSY statue scores. Future research should investigate gender and SES differences in the relationship between early childhood obesity and EF.

---

* The full version of this chapter can be found in *Child and Adolescent Health Yearbook 2015*, edited by Joav Merrick, published by Nova Science Publishers, Inc, New York, 2016.

† Corresponding author: Amanda K Brzozowski, PhD, MPH, Rollins School of Public Health at Emory University, 1518 Clifton Rd, NE, Atlanta, GA 30322, United States. E-mail: amandakbrzozowski@gmail.com.

SOCIAL DISORGANIZATION THEORY: AN EXAMINATION OF RACIAL HETEROGENEITY, RESIDENTIAL INSTABILITY, AND SOCIOECONOMIC STATUS*

Arielle Simmons, MS, and Michael E. Antonio†, PhD
West Chester University, Pennsylvania, US

Social Disorganization Theory (SDT) has been used frequently by social scientists to explain the occurrence of crime in an urban setting. Such environments are characterized by tough inner city streets, tight living quarters, and congested populations. Little evidence has been gathered, however, that extends the principles of SDT to urban settings that have few of these traditional features. The present analysis used available data to examine the impact of racial heterogeneity, residential instability, and socioeconomic status on incidents of criminal behavior, and specific crime types, reported in Chester County, Pennsylvania. While the county is classified as an urban dwelling, the region is characterized by multiple features that represent more of a suburban setting. Overall, findings from bivariate analyses showed indicators for racial composition, residential mobility, and social status lend support for SDT related to increased incidents of criminal behaviors; however, findings from multivariate analyses were less conclusive. Policy implications will be discussed.

* The full version of this chapter can be found in *Advances in Sociology Research. Volume 17*, edited by Jared A. Jaworski, published by Nova Science Publishers, Inc, New York, 2015.

† West Chester University, Department of Criminal Justice, 50 University Boulevard, Room 200-C, West Chester, Pennsylvania, 19383, email: mantonio@wcupa.edu.

Smoking, Socioeconomic Status and Health*

Lori J. Curtis, PhD†
Department of Economics, University of Waterloo,
Waterloo, ON, Canada

This chapter, like many others, attempts to document the association between smoking and health. Unlike other studies, we do not simply control for socioeconomic status by adding income and/or education and other control variables within a multivariate framework. Using the Canadian Community Health Survey, designed to allow pooling of samples over many cross-sections to achieve large sample sizes, we examine the relationship between smoking and health within socioeconomic classes defined by 40 sex-income-education strata. We question whether income or education may be more or less moderating in the smoking-health relationship. Our results clearly indicate strong relationships between smoking and self-reported health status for males and females across the 20 income-education strata. The picture is less clear when using self-reported chronic conditions for females and even less so for males. We find that, in the Canadian context, income is more 'protective' within education strata than education is within income strata indicating that the situations afforded by increased income may be more important for smoking-health relationship than the additional knowledge and productivity associated with higher levels of education.

---

* The full version of this chapter can be found in *Smoking Restrictions, Risk Perceptions and Its Health and Environmental Impacts*, edited by Nazmi Sari, published by Nova Science Publishers, Inc, New York, 2014.

† Phone: +1-519-888-4567 ext. 33162; Fax: +1-519-725-0530; E-mail: ljcurtis@uwaterloo.ca.

Socioeconomic Status and Health Implications*

I. C. Céspedes[1], *N. R. Oliveira-Monteiro*[2], *M. C. Garcia*[1], *D. A. Ribeiro*[1] *and R. C. Spadari-Bratfisch*[1]

[1]Department of Biosciences, [2]Department of Health, Education and Society, Institute of Health and Society, *Campus* Baixada Santista, Federal University of Sao Paulo, Santos, SP, Brazil

The socioeconomic status (SES) is considered a well-established risk factor for poor health, the poorer the SES the worse prospects for health outcomes. SES gradients in disease's risk are partially explained by bad health related behaviors, and partially by environmental conditions that people at lower SES are exposed to. Stressors whether they were physical or psychological, activate several neural pathways including the hypothalamus-pituitary-adrenal axis and the autonomic nervous system. The stress response aimed to create resilience and guarantee survival may then turn in mal-adaptation, increasing vulnerability to illnesses. One of the consequences is the increase in the cortisol plasma levels that superimpose to the endogenous corticosteroids circadian rhythm which might be altered by the low SES, as well as by an adverse work or domestic environment, conditions that determine chronic psychosocial stress, and contribute to the prevalence of severe illnesses. Indeed, negative correlations between monthly income wage and salivary cortisol levels were reported. When the SES is accompanied by additional stressors, the risk for diseases is accentuated and, in some cases, stress is characterized by hypocortisolism rather than hypercortisolism. High levels of epinephrine were also associated with low SES. These stress hormones effects on the brain and peripheral organs may trigger diseases to which the individual presents some genetic predisposition. Therefore, public policies that give social support to people living in low SES may impact positively on their health.

* The full version of this chapter can be found in *Socioeconomic Status and Health Implications*, edited by Sarah Reibert and Alice Jannings, published by Nova Science Publishers, Inc, New York, 2012.

The Impact of Low Socioeconomic Status on Child Mental Health and Strategies for Reducing Disparities Across Sectors of Care*

***Catherine DeCarlo Santiago*†,**
Sheryl H. Kataoka,
Jeanne Miranda
and Bonnie T. Zima

University of California, Los Angeles, Department of Psychiatry and Biobehavioral Sciences, Center for Health Services and Society, Los Angeles, CA, US

The link between low socioeconomic status (SES) and child mental health problems is well established. Nevertheless, the mechanisms underlying this relationship are multi-faceted and complex, involving factors at the child, parent, community, and system levels. For children living in low-income families, disparities in mental health are further accentuated by limited access to care, fragmented care, and poor quality of care. Thus, in this chapter we review the influential role of social determinants of mental health for children living in poverty. Next, we review disparities in mental health services access and utilization. Finally, we discuss strategies for reducing disparities among low SES children through interventions targeted to prevent, detect, and treat mental health problems within and across community-based care sectors serving low-income children.

---

* The full version of this chapter can be found in *Socioeconomic Status and Health Implications*, edited by Sarah Reibert and Alice Jannings, published by Nova Science Publishers, Inc, New York, 2012.

† Corresponding author, Email: csantiago@mednet.ucla.edu.

SOCIOECONOMIC STATUS AND INDIVIDUAL ADJUSTMENT IN EARLY ADOLESCENCE[*,1]

Massimo Santinello, Alessio Vieno[†]
University of Padova, Italy

Socioeconomic status (SES) has been shown to play an important role in socialization. In the present study three indicators of socioeconomic status were examined in terms of their relations with each other and three areas of social adjustment. The three measures of SES were: father occupation, Family Affluence Scale, and a single question regarding the individual's subjective evaluation of the family's SES. The social adjustment measures included school adjustment, parental support, psychosocial well-being, and two related behaviors health habits (physical activity, and dietary habits). The sample was composed of 3,168 Italian middle school students (47.3% girls). Bivariate correlations among the three measures of SES were weak, and only one of those measures (the subjective evaluation) was consistently correlated with adjustment. Using Structural Equation Models, however, showed that the different measures of SES could be used to create a latent construct of SES, which demonstrated a reliable relation with four of the five social adjustment constructs (school adjustment, parental support, and two health habits). Our results suggest that, in the study of social inequalities during adolescence, we need to consider indicators that could have a strong effect during the rest of the life. Moreover, comparing different type of analysis, the study offered a rationale for use SES in terms of a latent construct.

[*] The full version of this chapter can be found in *Socioeconomic Status and Health Implications*, edited by Sarah Reibert and Alice Jannings, published by Nova Science Publishers, Inc, New York, 2012.

[1] The HBSC study in Veneto is funded by Regione Veneto (D.G.R. n° 203 of April, 4, 2000). HBSC is a cross-national study co-ordinated from the European Office of WHO. International co-ordinator for the 1997/99 study: Candace Currie, University of Edinburg; Data Bank Manager: Bente Wold, University of Bergen; National co-ordinator: Franco Cavallo. University of Torino.

[†] Address correspondence to: Alessio Vieno. Department of Developmental and Social Psychology, Via Belzoni 80, 35131 Padova, Tel. ++39 049 8278479; Fax. ++39 0498278451 E-mail: alessio.vieno@unipd.it; Socioeconomic Status and Individual Adjustment in Early Adolescence.

INDEX

B

C

D

E

F

G

H

I

J

K

L

O

P

Q

R

S

T

U

V

W

Y